COMMUNICATION
FOR ENGINEERS

COMMUNICATION FOR ENGINEERS
Bridge that gap

7 DAY
BOOK

Richard Ellis
Consultant

A member of the Hodder Headline Group
LONDON • SYDNEY • AUCKLAND
Copublished in North, Central and South America
by John Wiley & Sons Inc.
New York • Toronto

First published in Great Britain in 1997 by Arnold,
a member of the Hodder Headline Group,
338 Euston Road, London NW1 3BH

Copublished in North, Central and South America by John Wiley & Sons, Inc.
605 Third Avenue, New York, NY 10158

British Library Cataloguing in Publication Data
A catalogue record for this book is available from the British Library

Library of Congress Cataloging-in-Publication Data
A catalog record for this book is available from the Library of Congress

ISBN 0 340 67718 X
ISBN 0 470 23760 0 (Wiley)

Produced by Gray Publishing, Tunbridge Wells, Kent
Printed and bound in Great Britain by J W Arrowsmith, Bristol

Contents

Acknowledgements

This book owes much to the close involvement of a number of staff from the Engineering Faculty of Heriot Watt University, Edinburgh who have kindly given of their time and expertise to assist the author. Particular thanks for their very helpful criticisms are due to Derek Fordyce (Senior Lecturer, Department of Offshore and Civil Engineering), Dr Patricia Erskine and Dr Bruce Davies (lecturers in the Department of Mechanical and Chemical Engineering) and to the many students and staff in the Faculty who provided ideas, examples of problems in communication, and their possible solutions.

The author would like to thank John Weitzen and James Reid for their contribution and to John Gilbert for his assistance in preparing the text.

Over a number of years the author has run courses in Effective Writing with the Ferranti company, now part of GEC Marconi Avionics in Edinburgh. Experience in teaching these courses has been of value in the writing of this book. Thanks are due to John Bishop (Training Department) for his assistance and to Charlie Napier (then Proposals and Documents Manager). The author acknowledges the help given by those who attended these courses for the many examples provided,

Finally, to Grace and Victoria for their help, tolerance and patience during the writing of this text, and to Charles for working on the index.

Part I

Part 1

1

Introduction

At 23 minutes and 4 seconds after 1 am on the 26th April 1986 an engineering experiment went badly wrong. Within minutes the reactor number 4 of the Chernobyl power plant exploded. It now appears that there was a failure of communication between those designers who wanted to carry out an experiment on number 4 reactor and the other engineers on site. No one appeared to have fully understood the risks involved in the experiment. It had not been done before. It seemed relatively straightforward. The designers appear not to have fully briefed their colleagues. The irony is that the experiment these designers were working on was to improve safety on the reactor!

The subtitle of this book is *Bridge That Gap*. The gap is to do with communication, not listening to what others say, not being able to read what others write, not being able to understand the terms in the report, and so on. The list is endless. The gap is sometimes wide and we can easily recognize it, as with the above case study, or it is narrow and we can easily miss it (well I thought it was obvious really!). We may not be involved in quite such dramatic and obvious gaps as those at Chernobyl, but all engineers have some rather special challenges in their day-to-day communication.

- The situations often worked in (such as nuclear reactors) are potentially hazardous. The consequences, therefore, of a communication failure are often greater than say in an office or college. *'The failure to maintain the pump resulted in a sudden surge of hot steam; this produced severe burns on the neck and face.'*
- Engineers are often working on-site with many others, all trying to complete the contract. Messages come on to the site and may become lost or scrambled in transmission. *'Message from Bob; he said that the figure you wanted was 10% for the first three months, OK?'* (In actual fact it was 10% for each of the first three months!)
- Engineers are often communicating off-site with non-engineers administrators, accountants, etc. They have to be able to translate engineering English into plain English. *'What this means is that the force on the sides of the structure will be roughly equal to that on the top. That's putting it at its simplest. Let me sketch it for you.'*

- Engineers are working under time pressure – contracts have to be completed; such pressures can make it less likely communication will be complete – short cuts may be taken. *'I tell you it's got to be finished by next week; there won't be much time for this meeting.'*

In view of this it is perhaps surprising that until fairly recently little attention was given to developing the communication skills of engineering students. Communication was rather left to take care of itself; students were assumed to be able to do it! The author has been involved in effective writing and communication courses with engineering companies over several years, but in some cases such courses have only recently been given greater emphasis. Many BEng and MEng courses have as part of their aims the development of transferable skills; communications being regarded as a key one. A recent report by The Engineering Council commented on the need to develop core communication skills in engineering students.

This increased interest and demand for training in communication reflects the fact that engineers are so much more involved in situations where they are required to communicate competently – such as the writing of a report, giving a presentation, summarizing material and negotiating. The attention given to such matters as total quality management increasingly involve engineers being asked to write audit reports, give briefings, and so on. The fact that competitive tendering is now the norm in so many areas means that engineers have to win business not only by the excellence of the designs and engineering work but by their ability to persuade, influence and present their ideas to win the contract. It was these needs which prompted the writing of this book.

One of the arguments often aired is that with the new generation of communication technology the need to develop interpersonal communication skills, the ones we focus on in this book, may become of less importance. The interactive video disk, the CD-ROM, the voice-in word processor, all mean that the built-in correction programs, the spell and style checkers, will take care of any slips that we might make. Increasingly sophisticated programs, according to this argument, will correct grammar, spoken and written, re-tune our communication to a necessary degree of formality, translate it into business French, adjust it so that it will slot into any application form, re-work it so that we can have the answers to any interview question, etc. Certainly such programs are being developed now and will increasingly be of help in some situations. However, we feel despite the development of video conferencing and the like, the real business will still get done face to face and engineers will still be judged greatly on their interpersonal communicative competence.

Although the main focus for this book is on the requirements of students taking engineering courses at university it is hoped it will also prove useful to practising engineers who have passed through their student days but are now grappling with many and varied communication challenges.

This book provides various approaches to communication: oral, non-verbal, written and graphical. There are a number of *examples* in the text. These are not intended as models in the sense that they represent the only way to write a CV, put together a report or plan for a presentation – they are there to provide you with a starting point, a map on which you can find your way.

There are a number of *activities*. These are points where you are encouraged to stop reading for a moment and think through an answer or your response to a question or problem raised. Then there are specific *exercises*. These are rather more cut and dried issues. You will find the answers to these at the back of the book. At the end of each chapter you will find the key ideas put in the form of a *summary* together with some further reading.

You will find some *examples* of work from engineers, both as students and those within practice. These have been adapted and the authorship obscured.

As you read the book you will find key ideas marked ❏. These are set out so that you can re-read the text and be reminded of them.

The plan behind the structure of the book is that we start with one to one, the interview, the telephone call, then move to communicating with groups and larger audiences. We move on the written word, graphical communication and aspects of the new technology of communication. Then we provide a tool box of useful and practical nuts and bolts of English usage – spelling, punctuation, grammar, symbols, signs, and so on. Finally there are the answers to the various exercises.

Making full use of this book

We all learn in rather different ways. But there is enough research now to suggest that there are at least two techniques which can considerably assist you in making the best use of this book.

- Try to *relate* the case studies, topical instances and examples to your own experiences. You may not have been involved in anything remotely connected with the actual situation as identified in the case study (i.e. not involved in a burning nuclear reactor!) but you might well have been in a situation where one team had not sufficiently well briefed the other (say in a sports situation – less dramatic, but of great importance for the players). People often complain that the trouble with books is that they don't teach you anything useful – that they're not related to the real world. Well, this one aims to be just that, but you can help by relating your experiences to ours. Try and link backwards and forwards from your experience of a situation to the case study and from the case study to your experience. This is why we also have the activities and exercises for you to try out; they are designed to help you consolidate ideas as well as provide that essential linkage.
- Try also when you have read a section to *reflect* a little on the merits of what was written in relation to your experiences. Reflective learning means that when we have an experience – a successful outcome or a more

negative one – then we don't just forget all about it but try to reflect on why it was either positive or negative and what lessons, if any, can be learned from it. For instance, when we come to discuss interviews and being interviewed for a job then this kind of approach is often sought by prospective employers. What lessons, they may ask, have you learnt from this particular experience?

So do try these approaches with this book.

Communication: one word but many approaches

Communication has become such a well-used word. We hear it in all sorts of contexts, everything from politicians' failure to communicate with the electorate to football managers being blamed because they can't communicate with their players, lecturers with their students, etc. We are bombarded by advertisers trying to persuade us that their particular product will enable us to be better communicators. We are told that we are in a communications revolution. However, consider those now in their 80s and 90s and the kind of communication upheaval they will have lived through – most of them were born before the telephone and radio let alone TV and satellite communication!

This is not the book to take these issues into the depth they require. As engineers, however, you should consider some basic models of the communication process. It was in fact two engineers working for the Bell Telephone Company in the late 1940s who devised a model of communication on these lines.

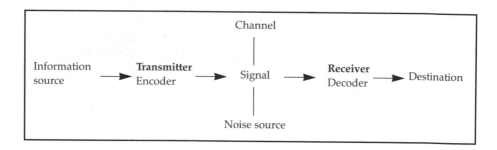

Although this is a very simplified model of what is a very complex communication process it did offer some interesting insights which we will be referring to in this book.

Channel. This refers to the way in which the message is sent – fax, telephone, face to face, written, smoke signals! We have divided this book into parts and these in some way represent these channels. However, it is worth saying at the start that books on communication increasingly stress the importance of interchannel communication. This is why you will find many cross-references in this book to material either already covered or that you will be meeting. It shows the richness and sheer diversity of communication processes.

Although we do not use the terms *sender* and *receiver* we do mention speaker and listener, interviewer and interviewee, writer, reader and audience. We shall be constantly emphasizing that communication does not happen in a vacuum. We can safely say that the vast majority of communication happens when one person sends and the other receives. Shannon and Weaver used the term receiver; this has a rather passive ring to it. We constantly emphasize the active listener and active receiver. We look in the next chapter at underlying attitudes and expectations; these are often the keys by which we can unlock active reception of a message. With these keys in place, we will be in a better position to tune and fine tune our communication so that it is more likely to be received and acted on.

The model uses the terms *encoder*, the one who puts the message into words, and *decoder*, the one who makes sense of these words. Much of this book will feature the responsibilities of making sure that the message sent is understandable to the audience. We examine issues therefore relating to plain English, the need for clear and unambiguous meanings and pitching the information at a level of technical sophistication appropriate to the recipient. We should as encoders not expect that our recipients will have to do too much to decode our meanings. Such activities may suit the heroes of a spy novel but when time is limited and the pressure of work grows we cannot afford to have to spend time figuring out (decoding) what meaning was intended. It was all very well for the poet James Joyce to spend the whole of one day working on three sentences so that every nuance and subtlety could be explored, but engineers need to make sure that what is said or written is immediately accessible and is not a puzzle to be decoded at length.

Shannon and Weaver mentioned *noise*. On the one hand this is a very important consideration if we take it literally. In other words we know that many communications are ruined because the line is noisy, there is just too much interference, too many distortions, wavy lines, loud noises, white noise and so on to make the message easy to attend to. They were right in getting us to take note of this and therefore to ensure that we do all we practically can do to reduce such distortion and disturbances.

One could argue that this kind of noise is fairly easily put right; it is the 'psychological' noise which is more difficult to counter (see Chapter 2).

Two other useful byproducts from that simple model of communication are the terms *redundancy* and *entropy*. In communication terms a redundant message is one that is highly predictable and very normal. This would be illustrated by the sentence: 'The engineer had to study maths to an advanced level'. However, if we wrote: 'The engineer had to study aromatherapy to an advanced level', this might cause us to pause a little. What, we would wonder, had aromatherapy to do with engineering. This sentence might make us sit up and take notice. Advertisers are continually constructing entropic messages. That is until these become stale and redundant, then they move on to something more entropic and unusual. We will be referring to these terms at a number of places in the book.

One of the aspects that Shannon and Weaver neglected in their model was that of *feedback*. We will be providing you with a number of references to the importance of obtaining feedback in the sections on making a presentation, interviewing, chairing meetings and letter writing. It is now considered an absolutely crucial component of any attempt to model human communication.

An equally powerful model, also from the late 1940s, is that of Laswell. He suggested that we should look at communication with the following questions in mind:

- *Who?*
- *Says what?*
- *In which channel?*
- *To whom?*
- *With what effect?*

Notice again the use of channel, but note the difference between the Shannon and Weaver and the Laswell model – the element of effect. In other words the simple model, the purely theoretical perspective is being replaced with notions of *effectiveness*. We all know that we can have a presentation which is incredibly slick and well prepared but because of some defect, some lapse, it is almost totally lacking in effect. No one feels inspired to do anything at the end. That obviously is one measure of effectiveness or lack of it!

Engineers cannot afford to ignore this aspect. They have to be conscious all the time of the effect of their writing and their words on others. They can't just hope that their fellow engineer has understood, has been listening or has read that specification. They have to be re-assured from the feedback obtained. They need to check for the effectiveness of their message.

Efficiency and effectiveness

Throughout this text we will be referring to the crucial distinction between *effectiveness* and *efficiency* of communication. An example may help make this distinction clear. An efficient communication could be, for instance, a manager making a presentation to all 150 members of staff on a planned change of policy within the engineering company. It is efficient because one person is speaking, the message is being relayed to all the staff at one place and at one time. To hold a number of small meetings all over the plant would be less efficient in terms of the manager's time and breaks in the work. However, we might want to question the *effectiveness* of this kind of communication. After all just how many staff will want to raise questions with the manager in that size group? If there are to be no questions, remembering our point about the active receiver, then just how much of that communication will sink in? What looks on the surface as a highly efficient communication in terms of costs, convenience, getting information to the largest number of people, when analysed, raises serious questions as to just how effective it has been in:

- providing them with key information
- changing people's minds, i.e. convincing them of a need for change
- making them more willing to embrace change, etc.

Then it might not be quite so effective!

Effectiveness and efficiency are part and parcel of any approach we may have to customer care. We shall constantly be emphasizing that your receiver is your customer. The engineer on the telephone you are speaking to is your customer in communications terms; that reader of the report you've written is again your customer. As with all customer care we need to:

- Consider our *customers' needs* – what does he or she want from this communication?
- Consider our *customers' expectations* – what do they expect from this communication?
- Consider the *customers' situation* – where is this customer in terms of previous knowledge about me and the contents of my message?

With these thoughts in mind we now examine some of the ways in which engineers can bridge the communication gap. We very much hope that having read this book you will be able to do some serious bridge building.

Summary

- Engineers are faced with constant challenges to their ability to communicate.
- The consequences for engineers who fail to communicate well are often profound and can have major impact on others.
- More attention is now being paid to the development of communication skills in engineering courses.
- Learning from a book such as this can be enhanced if the reader aims to relate it to personal experience, to reflect on the applications of theory to practice and on success and failure in communicating.
- Models of the communication process emphasize such components as receiver and sender, channel and noise. Feedback is a crucial component of any model of human communication.
- We need to constantly think about the differences there may be in efficiency and effectiveness of communication. We should be careful not to confuse these.
- We should apply customer care perspectives in our communications with others.

Further reading

R J Ellis and A McClintock (1994) *If You Take My Meaning*, 2nd edition. Arnold.
J Fiske (1990) *Introduction to Communication Studies*. Routledge.
D Mortensen (1972) *Communication*: *The Study of Human Interaction*. McGraw-Hill.

2

One-to-one communication
– attitudes and expectations
– the psychological aspects

Before getting into communication skills we explore the deeper aspects behind all communication – attitudes and expectations. We introduce you to notions of transactional analysis, aspects of language in communication and the importance of recognizing the cultural dimension.

Introduction

When an engineer communicates on the telephone, with a client or fellow engineer, we often think we can know what is happening. We can listen in on the conversation, we can record and analyse it. However, this is very different from running an experiment on the stresses caused to the leading edge of a wing in flight. We can take this wing and place it in a wind tunnel and examine through sophisticated experiments exactly what stresses are occurring.

Although we may be able to record the words in a telephone conversation we are not able, as in our engineering lab with sophisticated monitoring equipment, to get inside the skulls of the two conversationalists to find out what they are really thinking and feeling. For instance, consider this conversation set in a consulting engineers' practice.

JOHN *'Jill yes that's fine. I'm sure we can get this done in the time scale.'*
JILL *'Well that's great. I knew that I could rely on you.'*

So much for the actual words used but supposing we were able to get inside their skulls and find out their true feelings. We might be surprised:

JOHN *'Jill yes that's fine.'* (Oh my God does she realize what a fine mess we're in?) *'I'm sure we can get this done on time'* (If only you could really know the hassle this will give me! It'll be a miracle if we can get it done but I'd better not tell her the truth!)
JILL *'That's great'* (Well you really made a bodge of it this time.) *'I knew I could rely on you.'* (That's the very last time I'm allowing you on this

kind of project – he's always making some excuses and then we have this performance!)

From this analysis – not necessarily exaggerated – we can see what a gap there might be between what is said and what is actually meant.

On the printed page it is particularly difficult to bring out the full flavour of most interpersonal communications, what communication specialists would call the deep as opposed to the surface structure. However, by observation of the non-verbal expressions – Jill's distasteful expression (and she tries to hide it!) when John says: 'That's fine' – and by listening carefully to the para language, that is the tone and tune of the words and the amount of emphasis on a particular word, we could make a pretty shrewd guess at the true feelings of both parties. The point about these deep structures is that they are often well hidden and we have to listen and observe carefully to read the signs.

> ❏ Communication is not machine processed; it is not just the surface features that we need to attend to but the deep ones.

We don't have space to go into detail on these deeper aspects of communication – we refer you to books that do – but as engineers trying to bridge that gap with other engineers, and with non-engineers you ought to know a few key features of these deep structures.

Others' attitudes

Communication often fails not because it isn't carefully structured or accurate or well designed, but for the simple reason that it is not acceptable to the readers and listeners it is intended to appeal to. As we shall see when it comes to the preparation for a presentation to a group or a report to a readership, we have to probe behind the surface features and see what are the deeper attitudes.

Basically, we shall be working with three kinds of audience (we use audience in the widest sense in this book). It does not just refer to a group sitting listening to your presentation. On pages 72–75 we go into this in some detail under the topic 'Consider your audience when preparing your presentation'.

There are those that are *favourably disposed* to your message (and perhaps to you). If you find yourself communicating to such a positive audience then unless you run over time, use up too much paper, spend too long on their telephone, stray off the agreed topic, etc., you will normally get a good response.

Then there are those who are *basically neutral*. They wait to be convinced one way or the other, or they may just be apathetic. With these people you will have to prepare yourself carefully, make sure that you have all the necessary facts and figures, keep to the point, keep within agreed time and paper limits, provide a structure and a positive conclusion. Your aim is to stimulate latent enthusiasm, overcome lingering doubts and arrest their attention. You need to pitch your tone and style carefully. You must be aware of the dangers of patronizing or talking down to any audience.

Then unfortunately there are some who will be *negative* to your message and perhaps to you as someone who in their eyes represents the message. This negativity can be caused by all kinds of reasons:

- the audience may have suffered a poor service from your organization in the past
- they may have had a negative experience with the kind of material/ information/service that you are communicating to them
- they may have 'been got at' by someone (perhaps your competitor) and they have been provided with a negative impression
- they may be put off by your non-verbal behaviour – the gestures you make, the way you stand, slouch, etc.
- they do not like your language, its tone, the words you use, references you make, etc.

Given this long list, what can you do?

Well the simple answer is that first of all you need to be aware of and alert to the fact that such attitudes exist. If you have a rosy picture of yourself and the organization you represent, are involved in, and that doesn't square up to others' attitudes then you're in for a shock. This kind of shock can do great and even lasting damage to your confidence as a communicator.

The first thing is try and *assess* what the attitudes of your audience are likely to be. You can do this by asking people who have been in touch with them. Ask them what impressions they gained of the audience's mood, expectations, level of understanding, technical expertise, etc.

You need to put yourself in their shoes, to ask yourself: *'What would my attitude be if I were a member of this audience?'*

If you are in one-to-one communication you should be able to read their non-verbal signals and so react accordingly: if you are picking up signs that they want to leave and that they have had enough then bring the conversation/interview to a rapid close.

Having attempted to elicit what the attitudes are then you must seek to counter them. The first stage is to acknowledge them and the reasons behind them. It's no good plodding on pretending that everything's all right with the world when for them it plainly isn't. If you don't acknowledge their attitudes then they will probably not listen or pay attention to what you communicate. It's rather like when we are ill we go to our doctor having to some extent diagnosed ourselves. There is a great deal of research evidence to suggest that if the doctor we go to gives our self-diagnosis no attention at all – merely dismisses it with: *'Oh no it can't be that'*, then we are that much less likely to attend to what he or she says to us in the consultation. We may be so busy listening to our own thoughts and attempting to defend our views that we stop paying attention. This is why it is so important before you try and change attitudes that you are able to show that you have understood and appreciated them, but not necessarily share them.

When you prepare your interview, business letter, telephone call, etc. think of reasons why they, the members of the intended audience, should change their attitude. Hone your arguments, seek out credible proofs why they should attend to your case. Make sure that you have facts that are reliable, as evidence, the proof that may help to win over their scepticism, the argument that might just clinch the case.

The audience's expectations

Having examined the audience's attitudes we also need to think carefully about their expectations. Many communications fail for this one very simple reason: the audience are expecting something other that what they get. We shall be looking at this when we examine presentation to groups and report writing. We must be careful not to make too many promises which we will not be able to redeem. We need to ask these kinds of questions to our audience, our customers:

- What particular areas would you like me to concentrate on in this presentation?
- What would you like covered in this report; to what kind of detail?
- What aspects would you like covered in the interview?
- When I phone back what would you like me to have checked?

What we are talking about here is basically a form of customer care as we outlined in the introduction. In order to be successful in our communication we therefore need to tune what we say and do to our audience's expectations. This is not to say that we slavishly follow orders, but to be able to influence others we need to respect these expectations. We also need to influence these expectations, to negotiate more. This is why we spend time examining the skills of assertion and negotiation in the next chapter.

Language in the communication

The actual words that we use may appear to our listeners and readers to be creating barriers to understanding. We may use 'exacerbate' when we might use 'make worse' in the phrase 'these problems would be exacerbated if test borings are not completed'.

We need to be sensitive to the language levels and expectations of our receivers. There's little point in writing in very simple terms if our readers will appreciate and expect a more sophisticated treatment. On the other hand we should be very careful not to give the impression that we are more clever that we actually are by using the latest piece of meaningless jargon in order to impress our customers. The author might gain some further sales of this book if it was entitled: *An Interepistemological Construct of Paradigms in Communication for Engineers* just because it sounded important and learned. However it would put off an even larger number who would think: *no thanks!*

We should use jargon only to an audience who share our language. To do otherwise is asking for trouble. Not only will you annoy your reader but make it less likely that he or she will try to read further. Always remember to spell out the meaning of any jargon the first time you use it, and do supply a glossary. (See pages 218–220 in the Tool box.)

A phrase such as: 'ISO 9002 has been put in place throughout the plant to assist with TQM', may be perfectly understandable to many engineers but there will always be some who have either never heard of or have forgotten what TQM means – never mind ISO 9002. There is so much jargon being generated these days that we have always to keep a weather ear open to detect if we are creating a barrier (see page 78 for further discussion on this issue).

Tone in the communication

As communicators we have to stand back and consider how we 'sound' to others – 'where we are coming from' – using a modern phrase. We may be seen to be coming from an authoritative, 'parental' mode, tending to dictate to others, speaking from a lofty eminence, the top dog syndrome. We may not be aware of this and would find it rather a shock to be told this from those we are communicating with.

Parents, adults and children

This is not the place to go into a study of transactional analysis (TA). If you are interested in this approach we refer you to books that will take you through the theory and provide examples for you to consider. Basically and very much in a nutshell what TA puts forward is this. If we transact, that is communicate by word of mouth, written word, electronic communication, in such a way that it appears to our recipient that we are being the 'critical parent' then this will tend to evoke in them a 'child' response. This may reveal itself in anger, sulks, or withdrawal from the communication itself.

If you use a particular tone of voice or tone in your writing this may well trigger off this 'child' response. For example, if a manager says to a subordinate during an appraisal interview:

MANAGER *'First things first, Jones you seem to be late to work a fair deal.'*

Mr Jones is likely to react

JONES *'Well, that's not fair. I've only been late twice this month and for good reasons.'*

MANAGER *'It is fair; you're supposed to be here on time – you know that!'*

In other words the parental tone is implied in such usage as *Jones* (rather Mr Jones, or Bill); the opening of the interview by attacking from the outset with an accusation and by not appearing to listen or want to listen to the explanation. According to TA this tone of communication will almost invariably trigger off the hurt or angry 'child' as in Mr Jones' response: 'That's not fair'. (Refer to pages 40–41 for more detail on this in relation to interviewing.)

What, according to this theory, we have to do is to approach all our business and professional communication on very much an adult-to-adult basis. We should be careful to avoid a parental note – either by the words we use or the tone in which they are expressed. We also have to be sensitive to the actions we take.

Suppose Bill Jones had sent his manager a report and had waited a month before he got it back through the internal postal system of the engineering company they both work for. Bill Jones opens the envelope in some anticipation remembering just how much work he put into this report. He flicks through the pages and sees, scrawled in red ink at the bottom of the last page: 'Useful'. That's all, nothing more, no comment on his recommendations, the detailed costings, etc. This is a transaction in TA terms and a very parental one (notice the use of red ink and the possible memories invoked of school and teachers).

We shouldn't be surprised to learn that Bill Jones was tempted to behave like a child, i.e. throw the report into the nearest wastepaper basket or go storming up to the manager's office or simply sulk ('that's the last time I'm putting that kind of work into a report if that's all the recognition I'm getting').

TA is a powerful explanation as to why so much communication goes wrong. One reason why it is so powerful is that it recognizes the verbal and non-verbal aspects of interpersonal communication – the shout as well as the finger pointing.

We saw in Chapter 1 just how much can be at work beneath the surface of communication. This is why it is never enough just to learn the surface skills. We can be excellent interviewers in terms of using plenty of eye contact with our interviewee, asking the appropriate questions, looking as though we are listening intently, taking useful notes, checking on facts, summarizing and concluding well. We can do all that but still fail as a communicator because below this surface approach we are approaching the interview in a very parental way, our attitude and that of the interviewee are completely different as are our mutual expectations of the outcome. An appreciation of TA may help us to become more sensitive to a whole range of interpersonal communications.

Communication and culture

One very obvious reason why communication may fail is because there is a cultural gap between the two parties. If you have travelled overseas for work or holiday you may well have run into this kind of difficulty. It is a very important part of communications and one which is receiving increasing attention. We refer you to books which feature this aspect, but suffice to say here is that we need to be sensitive to different cultures and their ways of doing things. For instance, those from the Arab-speaking world tend to stand closer together than people from northern latitudes such as the Scandinavian and British. This may explain the discomfort that can be aroused when an Arab stands talking to someone not of his or her culture. The instinctive northern European reaction is to move away. This can then be misconstrued as a rude gesture, one which displays a lack of friendliness.

Likewise for an British engineer invited into the office of French counterpart (who he has never met before) to rush in shake him by the hand and say in a loud voice *'Bonjour Pierre'*, when even his wife doesn't call him that, is likely to cause a little alarm to his French colleague. Such informalities should come much later – if they come at all – in the acquaintanceship. The British engineer might be thought to be rather too forward and pushy and this might not be a good start to the negotiation of a new contract.

The author was conducting a seminar in India and as usual began with introductions:

> *'Well I'm Richard, can we have some names. Yes, can we start with you. What's your name please?'*
>
> *'Dr Shastri'*
>
> *'Fine, but what do your colleagues call you?'*
>
> *'Dr Shastri'*
>
> *'Do you have a first name we could use during the seminar. We will be together over several days.'*
>
> *'Dr Raj Shastri'*
>
> *'Thank you.'*

It was obvious that the cultural convention concerning names was not going to be broken. In some companies in Japan first names are sometimes only issued after the second glass of sake during an office party in the local, and certainly not in the office!

As an engineer you will often need to adapt your approach to communication with others – those of different cultures, different attitudes and those holding different expectations of the communication from you. In order to build a positive relationship with others and get them to tell you what bothers them, what they want, what their hopes are, we have to be sensitive to the signals they emit. These, often of a non-verbal nature, may indicate 'where they are coming from' and how far we can go to meet them. We will often have to re-tune our communicative approach to suit their needs. Just because they happen to speak excellent English doesn't mean that they will 'speak' our culture.

Let's continue the journey – bridging those gaps!

Summary

- Surface communication – the lines people speak and write – doesn't tell enough about the reality of communication which is taking place.
- We need to be sensitive to attitudes and expectations which influence how our communication will be received.
- Our audience's expectations are crucial in determining the effectiveness of communication.
- Communication may be perceived as being parental in tone; this will tend to trigger off child reactions. Hence we need to be sensitive to the tone of our communication.
- The culture in which the communication is set will influence many aspects of communication. We may need to adjust our style to make it more appropriate to that culture.

Further reading

G Burton and R Dimbleby (1988) *Between Ourselves*. Arnold.
G L Nemetz Robinson (1988) *Cross Cultural Understanding*. Prentice Hall.
G Janner (1988) *Janner on Communication*. Guild.

Part II

3

One-to-one communication

This covers responsibilities for communication, active listening as opposed to hearing, the importance of checking information and making sure your listener has grasped the key points. The importance of effective procedures for one-to-one communication are stressed.

Introduction

One of the key communication skills is being able to provide information through a face-to-face briefing. It sounds so natural – it's what we've been doing for years but in fact it's really quite difficult to do well. It is vital that engineers are successful at it. Most of you reading this will have encountered the following situation:

> The motorist is unsure which way to go. He slows the car to a stop at the edge of the street and winds the window down; a passer-by is attracted by his call. *'Excuse me. Can you tell me how I get to George Street?'* The passer-by provides an explanation: *'Keep going to the junction, go right and then first left, proceed until you get to the traffic lights and then it's on your left'.* The driver thanks him, winds the window up, pulls out and then at the junction drives right and first left. Within five minutes he is completely lost down a cul-de-sac.

Whose fault was it that he got lost? Presumably the motorist's for not checking. He thought he was following the explanations, that is until he went down the wrong road! Was it the responsibility of the passer-by for not noticing that the driver looked rather worried and unsure during the explanations and therefore doing something about it – such as repeating a key phrase, sketching out something on the back of an envelope that he happened to have in his pocket?

Responsibility for communication one-to-one

We do tend to place most responsibility for one-to-one communication with the initiator – the person who does the talking. After all he or she is the one who gets things going – starts the ball rolling. It's his or her job to get the nature of the message over clearly. However, all too often the speaker is not sure what has to be said. This usually results in muddle and hesitation.

> ❏ It is essential to think through what you want to say and the order in which you need to say it.

Imagine the situation. In the office the chemical engineer Liz is briefing her junior colleague Jim.

LIZ *'Jim, have you got a moment?'*

JIM *'OK, no problem.'*

LIZ *'You know I'm going to be away until next Friday so I just want to run over some key points. I'm sorry, we should have had this talk much earlier but I've been busy.'*

JIM *'Fine, you go ahead.'*

LIZ *'Now it's important that when I'm not here next week that you check all the labs carefully and that experiment in lab two is reported on by Monday. You remember we spoke of that earlier.'*

JIM *'OK?'*

JIM *'Yes ...'*

LIZ *'And please don't forget that by Wednesday you'll need to have phoned the results of the tests for Mr Williams. OK?'*

JIM *'Yes ... em ...'*

LIZ *'Remember on the Tuesday or is it Monday – I'll have to check that – we've got that visitor from Malaysia coming round the plant and he may want to see around here. Well I think that's all.'*

JIM *'Yes ... well ... OK ... I'll handle it.'*

Activity

What advice would you give to Liz in the way she briefed her colleague? Compare yours with the advice underneath.

- She should have structured what she was going to say in her briefing. There should have been some kind of order (Now ... to ... Then, for instance).
- As she was briefing Jim, she should have paused and checked back to see if her message was getting through.
  It's far better if the other person has questions for you that he or she asks them there and then rather than having to wait until you've finished, by which time the point may have been forgotten.
- She should have made sure that her an oral briefing was backed up with a written one. She should either have given Jim a note of the key points there and then, or sent these to him soon after the briefing, certainly before

she had to leave so if there had been any uncertainty he could have got back to her in time.

People very quickly forget what they've heard unless they repeat it (like your telephone number) or if it is considered of crucial importance, or is made to stand out in some way from the remainder of the briefing – the speaker's use of emphasis for instance.

Let's see how that original briefing might have been improved.

LIZ   *'Jim, have you got a minute?'*

JIM   *'Sure, I've got to get to the stationery store by 11 to pick some materials but OK for ten minutes or so.'*

LIZ   *'That's fine, thanks. You know that I'll be away until Friday lunchtime. I suggest we sit down and I run through with you some key points to check while I'm away. I've written these down and here's your copy. So let's run through them.'*

JIM   *'Can I just check that you definitely won't be returning till next Friday at noon?'*

LIZ   *'Yes that's so. OK shall I go on?' Let's run through the list ... remember to check all the labs carefully. That experiment in lab two needs to be reported on by Monday the 7th at the latest. OK. I've put that down on this list but any problems?'*

So it continues. What a difference. There's nothing taken for granted here. Communication is seen as the slippery thing that it is – like a bar of soap in the shower – it needs to be firmly grasped. Jim isn't taking anything for granted. He checks back to make certain he's got it right and that he fully understands his responsibilities. When the Channel Tunnel was being constructed it was a disciplinary offence for a French engineer to walk away from a briefing with his British counterpart if he was in any way confused or unsure following the briefing and vice versa with his compatriot. No one gains if people leave a briefing still confused or unsure as to their responsibilities.

Active listening; it's hard work

Jim, in our first extract, might have looked as though he was listening, but he wasn't an active listener. By this I mean making sure that he didn't miss anything, making sure that if he was getting lost (like our motorist) he didn't wait until it was too late and so got stuck. The important thing is to do something.

- Ask a question?
- Repeat a point made.
- Take a note.

- Ask for a note.
- Ask for a summary.
- Provide a summary.
- Ask for a diagram.
- Provide a diagram.
- Ask for a delay while you get your act together.
- Check and check again if you're not sure.

This is being *assertive*. It is saying to the speaker: 'I have some rights in this matter. If I don't understand then there may be trouble for both of us. It's in both our interests to clarify what you mean. My questions might help you to clarify things, they might identify gaps in the information, which until you started to give the briefing you failed to realize. If I hadn't checked with you those experiments in the lab when you went through them on that list, then we could well have had a nasty accident.'

Naturally when the speaker is your manager, a person who holds some power that you do not have, then it is much more difficult to be assertive in these situations. It is all about how you say it; the tone of voice in which you are assertive. *'Excuse me could I just say at this point ...'* is likely to be more effective than, *'Hold on ...'.*

> ❏ Communication is what happens between a speaker who understands what he or she wants to say and a listener who takes some responsibility for capturing the meaning.

An active listener can also help a hesitant or unprepared speaker by not jumping in and interrupting the train of thought – that's being just too active – but by providing the clues which indicate that he or she is actually paying attention. This can make any speaker's job so much easier. It comes down to certain non-verbal behaviours. These could include:

- Making reasonable eye contact with the speaker (think just how off-putting it is when your listener is looking over your shoulder).
- Adopting a posture which doesn't distract, such as fiddling with a pen, constantly swivelling round, and so on.
- Avoid a pained expression: there's nothing more off-putting for a speaker to see the other person's not-very-interested expression.

In engineering it is vital to establish procedures for checking that what has been said has been fully understood. This is called feedback. Put simply it means: does the sender of the message – in this case our speaker – have some kind of acknowledgement that (a) the message has been received and (b) understood?

> The staff who needed to see the regulations for testing signals were not required to acknowledge receiving them to save 'administrative effort'. A

signal engineer said he was responsible for monitoring the way the instructions were being carried out. He had assumed the new rules had been received by everyone and were being implemented. (Official Inquiry into the Clapham Rail Disaster.)

We make such assumptions at our peril.

Can you think of any situations where you might have run into this kind of error – sending a message and not bothering to find out if it had in fact been understood (the other person had also acted on the assumption that you didn't need such acknowledgement). We shall have more to say on this topic of active listening in our next chapter.

The new technologies of communication such as e-mail, fax and the mobile phone should, in theory, make this process of acknowledgement easier. 'Just fax back and say OK.' No longer do we have to wait for that letter of acknowledgement or hope that the person will be able to borrow someone's office phone. With e-mail and other forms of organization-wide electronic communication the feedback system is fine but what happens when people start switching off their systems to get some peace from the continual hum and white noise of the computer? What happens when the systems get so clogged up with personal and trivial messages that we do not notice the key one which does in fact demand our response? We cannot assume feedback will by itself occur, we have to ensure that it does. We have to insist that it happens. We have to make sure that there are systems for providing speedy acknowledgement to the sender of the message. We examine some of these in our discussion on electronic communication, see pages 196–199.

Now let us have a look at some particular forms of one-to-one communication. Some of these will be familiar to you but you may not have seen them presented in this way. But first we provide you with some advice on negotiation and assertive behaviours.

Summary

- In any assessment of the success or otherwise of a one-to-one communication we need to remember that part of the responsibility for that success or failure lies with the listener, the recipient.
- It is vital that he or she checks the incoming information and if it is not clear asks questions, and makes every effort to clarify it.
- This is the concept of the active listener; it is a very much more energetic role than being a passive hearer.
- By being an active listener this may assist the communicator clarify his or her message.
- We need to try and get feedback on our messages. It is dangerous, particularly in engineering, to assume that just because a message has been received it has been understood. Furthermore, we cannot assume that because the message has been electronically sent it has actually be 'received' and understood.

Further reading

G Burton and R Dimbleby (1985) *More than Words*. Arnold.
N Stanton (1982) *What Do You Mean Communication?* Pan.

4

Negotiation, assertiveness and active listening

We examine various techniques for improving our assertiveness and our skills in negotiation. We take up and develop the theme of active listening.

Introduction

You probably associate negotiation with trade union leaders seeking pay rises, with bosses or government officials huddled in small rooms locked in debate over the size and shape of the European banana. Well we want to describe another kind of negotiation – the one with a small 'n'.

Suppose you are due to hand a piece of work – a project of some kind – to your tutor or client. You are running late (surprise). It is based on a number of lab experiments and you have had difficulty in getting all the results in on time. So what happens, do you panic or try and negotiate?

You panic! But after reading this chapter you go along prepared to negotiate.

You go and make an appointment to see the tutor or client – here we have the first principle of negotiation:

> ❏ If you don't ask, you don't get.

So many people give up at the first hurdle. Armed with this advice you go into this person's office and ask. It doesn't guarantee that you will always be successful but do ask. This leads us to the second important principle of negotiation which is:

> ❏ At the heart of every negotiation is an exchange.

You may ask what is there in the way of an exchange in this situation? Well your tutor will want the project in to complete his or her lists and you want a grade, some kind of formal recognition for the work you have done. You will hope that he will allow some softening of the final date for handing in and you in your turn will offer some kind of exchange. You might like to deliver it personally to his home, send it by express delivery, and so on. We must admit there isn't much to negotiate in this example but the principle is there.

Negotiation is often based on the idea of 'cards in the hand'. You need to think before you go into any of these situations what particular cards you have to play. Certainly in this one there are few, if any, aces. It's not as though you could refuse to hand over the project! Good negotiators also prepare carefully before they go into any negotiation. They consider what cards they have and what their bottom line is. This a yet another of those vital principles:

> ❏ Prepare before you negotiate; have a bottom line.

The bottom line is that point below which you will not want to go in your dealings – the unacceptable. It is a very important consideration when it comes to being assertive. One of the reasons why people are not assertive in many situations is that they can't say **no** (this is my bottom line and anything beneath it I will not put up with). Because there is no firm 'bottom line' then they are easily influenced and persuaded to accept a situation which afterwards they regret. For example, you want to sell that audio system and you've set £250 as the price to offer; you need to go into that negotiation with a bottom line (say £185) which represents your absolute limit. If you are offered a price lower than that it might be worth keeping the system for spares. This then is your bottom line. Having it clearly in mind will strengthen you in any negotiation; it will help you to be assertive. You will then be in a better position to resist being offered £85 and having to accept it.

We shall be saying more about being assertive later in this chapter.

There's one more important principle of negotiation before we go on to examine some actual situations: no matter how formal or informal the negotiation you should always try and distinguish between the other person's *stance* and his or her real *position*. In many traditional negotiations for instance, it is wages that form the principal bone of contention in the negotiation, but on careful listening and reading of the situation it becomes very apparent that there is something underneath this concern – it may be concerned with status and comparisons with others. So often what people say they want is not actually what they really do want. They will start with an opening and then if the other person actually listens something else may emerge – their true position. So

> ❏ Listen for the other party's true position as against the opening stance.

Now we have established some of the key principles, let's have a look at a situation where negotiation is being practised.

The scene is one where Jane Bolt, senior analyst with Cluedo Energy Consultants (a company that specializes in running energy audits with large companies) is talking with Harry Jones, General Manager with the Hot Bite biscuit factory.

GENERAL MANAGER | *'Well what do you think? You've seen our figures – how much we're spending on gas and electricity. Can you suggest any savings?'*

ANALYST | *'Well I'd like to give these figures a more in-depth analysis and spend some time with one of your senior engineering colleagues, then have a more detailed examination of the key areas.'*

GENERAL MANAGER | *'But even from your initial survey, do you think you can save us money?'*

ANALYST | *'Well I will say that we've experience in reducing costs in companies of your size.'*

Comment

In terms of negotiation the General Manager is trying to get the Analyst to commit herself; she is being cautious. She is keen to delay any verdict until she has the facts.

GENERAL MANAGER | *'Well from your experience what kind of savings could we expect after carrying out the kind of survey you're suggesting.'*

ANALYST | *'Well between 5–15%, but as I say I couldn't be more precise at this time without more analysis.*

GENERAL MANAGER | *'If we decide to go ahead what time scale are we in for?'*

ANALYST | *'If we received the go ahead from you within a fortnight then we could let you have an interim report within a month.'*

GENERAL MANAGER | *'And the final one?'*

ANALYST | *'That would depend on the level of detail.'*

GENERAL MANAGER | *'Well could we look towards the end of June?'*

Comment

Again the Analyst is being cautious. She does not want to over promise and then have to 'under perform'. 'Depend on the level of detail' signifies this sentiment.

ANALYST | *'That would be possible – it might stretch to the middle of July.'*

GENERAL MANAGER | *'So by the end of July at the latest we could expect to have the final report. I'm sorry to press you but we have a Board meeting at the beginning of August and I would be keen to share this information with my fellow directors. Now as to fees. I have read your prospectus. I take it then you would levy a 12% fee on all the savings you make for one calendar year and 8% for the second. Yes?'*

ANALYST   *'Yes, this is general practice.'*

Comment

We are now into negotiation over price. These are bargaining positions. If I do this for you, then can you do this for me?

GENERAL MANAGER   *'Are there exceptions?'*

ANALYST   *'Well, that would depend on the precise nature of our agreement.'*

GENERAL MANAGER   *'For instance?'*

ANALYST   *'Well, for instance if you wanted us to take on a further audit such as your use of telephone and fax. If you agreed we'd be in a position to offer you a reduction in normal fees.'*

GENERAL MANAGER   *'Yes, I see ...'*

ANALYST   *'Well why don't I put some figures together on this one?'*

GENERAL MANAGER   *'Yes, OK that could be useful. We've been conscious for some time about the costs in this area.'*

Comment

We are now getting to the deal. The General Manager is sending buying signals – there may be more business – but wants some movement over price. The Analyst is sending out positive buying signals: 'We'd be in a position to offer you a reduction on fees'. This is beginning to look like a deal.

We've indicated the key aspects of negotiation in this exchange. Both sides have 'won': the General Manager has gained commitments to dates and costs and the Analyst has left open slightly the date for the completion of the final report and has also put down a marker for further business with this particular organization. Both sides have set up markers for future dealings.

Remember we're after a win/win situation. The General Manager wants to gain the most savings from this survey and the lowest possible costs from the factory. The analyst wants to gain the largest slice of business possible and to gain further fees. Now you've read this consider the following:

- Situations where you were in a negotiating situation? (You probably didn't realize it at the time.)
- Situations where you were bargaining? (Remember everything is negotiable.)
- While bargaining did you think of your bottom line? (The walk away position?)

Assertiveness

You know the scene. You've ordered the meal, you've had the first course and have started the main one. The waiter comes round and asks 'Is everything OK?' You have not really enjoyed the food but what do you do? Do you put down your knife and fork and say to the waiter. 'No I'm afraid things are not OK.' If you're like most people you say 'Fine' and carry on eating and then reluctantly pay the bill.

In most interpersonal communication we have three options if we are not happy with things and wish to complain. We can:

- Remain passive.
  Merely shrug our shoulders and let things carry on. We justify this behaviour in this way: It's not really our business and besides nothing much happens if you do make a complaint. It only creates fuss and bother and can take a lot of time.
- Become aggressive.
  Make a fuss. Raise our voices – insist on action. *Waiter! Over here!*
- Act assertively.
  Make the complaint in a calm ordered fashion.
  'Excuse me, but I'm afraid the food was cold when it was served and I did ask for medium cooked steak and this is rare. Could we have replacement for this and the cold food.'

This is assertive behaviour. It sets out the issues – without aggression or passivity. It suggests that you as a customer of this restaurant have rights and that these have been ignored. It further suggests that if waiters go round asking if things are 'OK' then it is not unreasonable if things are not OK if the customer responds to that effect? You do wonder whether in some restaurants waiters actually believe in this message – perhaps it has become something of a ritual?

Assertive behaviour signifies that everyone has rights and if those rights are ignored, trampled on, then everyone in the situation suffers, the person and any others involved in the communication. In our example of the poor food in the restaurant then if assertive behaviour results in the customer being happy and the chef and waiters finding out how their service has fallen short and can be improved, then both parties benefit. You could in fact argue that future customers as a third party will also benefit.

Consider those situations where you have acted assertively and those where you acted passively or aggressively? Why did you decide to act assertively and what were the benefits?

Training in assertiveness is now a big business. You may well find yourself on a course. Engineers need to be assertive with other professionals they will be working with. Many engineers have perhaps not been as assertive as they needed to be because communication skills were never developed during training. Some engineers came into situations where assertive behaviours were called for but they failed to act assertively because it was not deemed appropriate so to do. Perhaps in the past there may not have been enough role models to learn from.

Listening

You my think it strange that we've returned to listening in this section, but as we've mentioned already a successful negotiation of any kind, whether over the reluctant handing in of a late project or a million pound engineering task, will require close listening in order to tease out the other party's real position as opposed to the stance they adopt. Listening is an integral part of assertive behaviour. We cannot act assertively unless we have thoroughly listened to the other person's point. A failure to listen and we can appear to be aggressive to the other party. *'Don't bother with that. I know all about it'.*

But what is listening? Have any of you ever been out walking with a bird watcher. Suddenly in the middle of a field or half way along a path, the bird watcher stops, freezes stock still and remarks, 'that's the lesser spotted twitter twat'. We may all the time have been aware of this warbling going on in the background but we weren't actually listening to it. That's basically the difference between listening and hearing.

> ❏ To recap: Listening is an active business, it implies concentrating on what is being said, while hearing is a much more passive affair, taking general note but not really following proceedings in any depth.

In our next chapter we will be looking at interview skills. This is one situation where it is of crucial importance to listen carefully.

A great deal has been written on the subject of listening. There are suggestions for further reading at the end of this chapter, suffice to say that here are some key principles for engineers.

• It's much better for both parties to do some negotiation before listening actually starts. If you phone someone in another office you don't know unless you use a video phone just how busy that person is and how convenient or not it really is for you to call. So negotiate. Try saying: *'Is this a convenient time to call or would you like me to phone later?'* You may, through your call, be bursting in on someone's work or leisure and, although you can pick up a great deal from the sound of their voices – the tone of irritation or disappointment – you may not appreciate just how far you are actually causing an interruption.

Very few people associate listening with negotiation and being assertive. We suppose that is because very few people think of themselves as negotiators.

We've shown you that negotiation is all about trying to make sure that your interests are respected and that you respect the interests of others. Listening, when it is effectively done, allows those speaking to feel safe.

Activity

Here's a typical situation that you would be able to find in any engineering office. As you read it through ask yourself: what does it tell us about negotiation and listening?

Harry, who is the senior partner with Rivet and Rust Engineers, is wandering along the corridor with something on his mind. He notices that the door to one of his more junior colleagues is open. He enters:

HARRY 'Have you got a minute?'
DAVID 'Well ... yes. Is it important?'
HARRY 'I'd like to pick your brains regarding this city hospital refurbishment project'
DAVID 'Well I haven't given it much thought ...'
HARRY 'You see the tender specified that all ...'
DAVID 'I haven't actually seen that tender so ...'
HARRY 'That's OK I just want to see what you think we should do with the time frame. It's going to be very difficult to complete all the surveys before April. Should we say outright that we don't think it's very realistic ...'
DAVID 'Well perhaps we should be a little more cautious about being so forthright ...'
HARRY 'Well, what do you suggest?'
DAVID 'Well, as I said I'm not too certain about the detail of this particular tender ...'
HARRY 'Oh Lord. I'd better find someone else.'

What did you think were the problems here? David, it was obvious, was a very unwilling participant in this discussion. He probably sent out strong non-verbal signals to his boss that (a) he was busy and therefore didn't relish being interrupted and (b) didn't know much about what was going on and therefore was not a very willing participant in the discussion. However, his boss did not pick up the cues. The situation then wasn't very conducive for good listening. With a little bit of negotiation and more assertive behaviour then this might have been the result.

HARRY 'Have you got a moment?'
DAVID 'I'm actually in the middle of something just now, could I come back to you on it?'
HARRY 'I wanted your ideas on this hospital refurbishment tender.'

DAVID   *'I've only skimmed it. Why don't I have a good read later today – I should have some time. Perhaps we can meet early tomorrow. Did you want me to look at any thing in particular?'*

HARRY   *'Well, yes, have a look at that section on time scales. I think it's going to be very difficult to get everything ready for April.'*

DAVID   *'Fine, I'll do that. Shall we say 9.30 in your office.'*

HARRY   *'Make it 10.00 would you?'*

DAVID   *'OK.'*

Some of you reading this, those with no experience of negotiating and being assertive, will think this sounds a little cheeky coming from a junior to a more senior person. But what are the gains from this kind of behaviour?

- David isn't having to pretend to have read the document. Secondly, he has negotiated some time to read it and therefore prepare his response. This is likely to be much more useful to both parties.
- David is also sending quite a powerful signal to his boss that he has his own work to do and anyone who interrupts may well reduce his effectiveness. It is in the interests of everyone in an organization to ensure that their work is effective. We often have to 'educate' our bosses, managers, tutors, colleagues and friends who may call us up in the middle of something or come into our rooms or offices for a chat, that we are in fact busy and need to finish a job.

How does this relate to listening? It's very difficult to listen if you don't feel comfortable, by this we don't just mean the quality of the armchair or the provision of that ice cold drink – although these can be very important – we mean do you feel safe listening – safe in that you understand what is going on and therefore feel confident to speak. This will come up when we look at seminars and communicating with groups (see pages 57–58).

What David did in that second scenario was to clear himself some space for listening. When he goes with the report in hand, having presumably read it and noted his boss' concerns, he will be able to focus in on listening. What he was doing in that first scenario was hearing – passive hearing. Harry should have picked up the non-verbal body clues which can normally warn us that the other person is not listening or does not want to listen. We have to be aware of body clues. Some people are rather deaf to such clues and it may be that if someone is more senior to the other then these are disregarded as a matter of course.

This is why we cannot rely on the simple sending out of non-verbal essages – we have to say something. We must assert ourselves in a polite way when someone says, *'Oh have you got a minute?'* or, *'You have got a minute haven't you?'*. We need to be able to say, not aggressively *'No'*, but, *'well I'm rather tied up just now.'* This is in fact buying space so that both parties can really listen.

Other key aspects of listening

- Try and clarify what it is you're supposed to be listening to – in other words avoid finding yourself just sitting absorbing a mass of information and not knowing where it comes from or why you should in fact be listening to it? The longer you leave it the worse it will be. We will see in our section on the participants' roles at meetings (pages 83–85) just what can be done in terms of asking for clarification of the remit. Here are some phrases that we can use:
  - *Can I just clarify what my role is here*
  - *Before you go on could I ask ...*
  - *Sorry, could I ask for a recap on what was decided last time.*
  We'll see in the section on meetings that these are also the kinds of questions that we need to ask when we are sitting in any kind of meeting or seminar.
- Try to summarize as you go along. This as we will see is a very important duty of any discussion leader or chairman. But if you can do this then you will find not only that it helps you listen but also enables others to keep a check of where everyone is.
- Try and have some kind of recording system. Take a few notes – bullet points – as you go along. Many of you will already do this when you are sitting in lectures. We look at note taking on pages 129–134. The important aspect about listening is to provide yourself with a record of the key points as you heard them.

  One of the great problems we all face when we are listening is that so much flows over our heads – it then disappears into thin air unless we make some kind of recording. The other benefit that note taking confers is that by making a summary we cannot only assist ourselves but also help the speaker – he or she may well feel relieved that we are bothering to make a note; we can assist this by summarizing the main points at the end. It is a principle of all good negotiation that there should be a summary of the key areas agreed as well as those which remain outstanding.

- Finally, do provide some kind of feedback to your speaker. Questions as outlined above are useful but apart from those which clarify you could pose others, for instance:
  - Expansion questions: *'Does that also apply to Chemical Engineers?'*
  - Checking questions: *'You said 4% over the contract price?'*
  - Closed questions: *'Was it the only time the pump failed?'*
  - Open questions: *'Could you indicate how quality could be improved?'*

It is the quality of the questions rather than the mere quantity of them that will indicate to the other person in the communication that you have been paying attention. As we have said both sides in an interpersonal communication have a responsibility to ensure that successful communication takes place. Remember Chernobyl!

We now examine a key aspect of one-to-one communication – the interview. This is a setting where great care is needed by both parties to listen, negotiate and on many occasions behave in an assertive manner.

Summary

- Negotiation skills and approaches are there to be used by anyone to assist us in our one-to-one communications.
- Negotiation is all about an exchange, one in which both parties win.
- To be effective in a negotiation you have to prepare your 'case'.
- Assertiveness is all about protecting your rights; passivity is when you lose your rights and aggressive behaviour is when you take over someone else's rights.
- Effective listening is vital in a negotiation since you need to fully understand the differences between a position and the true interests of the other party.
- We need to attend carefully to others' body language clues for information as to their true feelings so that we can adjust our communication.

Further reading

G Burton and R Dimbleby (1988) *Between Ourselves*. Arnold.

R Fisher and W Ury (1988) *Getting to Yes. Negotiating for agreement without giving in.* Houghton Mifflin.

J C Freund (1992) *Smart Negotiation: how to make deals in the real world.* Simon and Schuster.

T Harris (1970) *I'm OK – You're OK.* Pan Books.

5

The interview

We look at some of the most common types of interview that you will be involved in. Success at an interview, whether that be selection, appraisal, disciplinary or market survey depends a great deal on key communication and interpersonal skills. We look therefore at some specific aspects of listening and body language – some of which we have previously mentioned but bring them together here to show the degree of interrelationship between them.

Introduction

The interview, how terrible that sounds; it often represents a kind of Spanish Inquisition: grim faces looking at you from behind a series of double-breasted suits and a large formal room. It will be a series of traps – they'll ask you to sit and there's no chair, they'll pose all those trick questions!

We would like in this section to turn this nightmare round and see it as an opportunity for you rather than a threat.

Apart from selection interviews we will examine other kinds of interviewing that engineers are involved in, such as those relating to obtaining information from a client. Much of what we say will also be of use when or if these are already part of your work.

We start with selection interviews – this is probably the one that is closest to your heart – you may in fact be thinking about going for one, you may have just filled in an application form and even now be awaiting the call, or you may have been interviewed for that most desirable post, only to receive that most bland and disappointing of all communications – the rejection slip.

Selection interviews

What is the purpose of a selection interview? From the point of view of the organization it is to select the right person for the right job. From the applicant's point of view it is very much about allowing him or her to make sure that it is the right choice at the right time in their lives.

Very often applicants let themselves drift into a job. This happens all too frequently, one can understand why, the pressure on young people is to get a job and therefore many will go for a post which in their heart of hearts they do not actually think is for them but they are pushed on by peer pressure. There is as much, even more pressure, for those out of work trying to get back in. You may have experienced the signs during the interview of that sinking feeling that indicates: *'This isn't for me!'*

It takes a considerable amount of self-confidence to be able to say to the interviewer or the panel, *'I now feel as we have been talking that I'm not probably the right one for this post.'* If this sounds a little too assertive then just consider what the consequences might be if you don't say anything and then are offered the job which you then get bored by and do badly in.

> ❏ An interview has two very definite purposes: to allow the organization to find the most suitable person for the vacancy that has been identified and secondly, to allow the candidate to find the opening which will best suit him or her.

> ❏ There is the absolute need to do your preparation about the post you are going for and the organization you are wishing to join.

A lack of preparation will most certainly show itself during the interview and will make you as a candidate that much less sharp and attractive. You can use all kinds of sources to assist you in this search: local newspapers, national press and media, local public library, reference books, etc. You can use these to determine: the size of the organization; what is its principal business; how many branches it has; whether it has recently amalgamated with another organization, etc. Increasingly organizations will send out briefing papers to provide you with some background for the organization. Do read these carefully. Potential employees are often expected to have some commitment to the ethos, the mission of the organization they hope to join. Don't go into the interview vague about this. Bone it up.

Remember that an interview just doesn't happen in isolation – there is a build up which may consist of the following stages.

Firstly, telephone calls from the organization you are applying to. These are increasingly common now. The advert will invite the applicant to phone up for further details. This has a twofold purpose: first, to allow you, the candidate, to ask further questions about the job and second, to provide a chance for that representative of the organization to find out a little more about you. It is a kind of selection barrier. A candidate who sounds lacking in commitment or interest or who fails to ask sensible questions about the organization he or she is applying for is less likely to be sent an application form. Organizations are increasingly trying to cut down on the immense amount of paper that comes flooding to them after they have placed an advert.

Secondly, assuming that you have successfully negotiated the first hurdle you now move on like a horse in the Grand National to the second of the fences – namely the application form or curriculum vitae (CV). Turn to page 116 for further details on how to prepare yourself.

There is an enormous number of books on the market which are designed to assist you in the interview. We've provided you with a selection at the end of this chapter. Here is some advice which could help you. But no money back promises if they don't work for you!

Third, assuming that your CV or application form has been successful in letting you past that hurdle – now to the interview. Here is a checklist:

- As soon as you get the details, write to confirm the time and the place.
- Check very carefully the exact part of the organization where the interview will be – don't assume because you have passed by the premises of the firm that it will necessarily happen there. You may find that for this interview they have taken over a hotel room, or another part of their organization further out of town.
- Take no chances with getting to the place well on time. Aim to be there 20 minutes early. By so doing you won't be arriving all flustered, hot and bothered and too breathless to answer the questions. If you have to drive there then double check the route and see what is said about parking. If nothing is written in the letter then work out where you will park. If going by bus or train then double check that the times you've written down don't apply to Saturday or peak periods. We may seem to be stating the obvious here but so many promising applications have been let down because the candidate arrived late, got lost, and therefore made a poor impression.
- Take a careful look at your surroundings. As you go into the reception area have a look at what is up on the walls, glance through a company newsletter which may have been left lying around. You may be able in your answers to make mention of some topical issue, this will show that you have attempted to get abreast of things. Don't take this business too far, we'd hate to see you arrested for industrial espionage as a result of reading this chapter!
- Jot down two lists of questions. The first will be those that you expect to be asked. These may include:
  - *Why are you applying for this particular post?*
  - *Why now?*
  - *Why are you leaving your present post (if relevant)?*
  - *How do you see your career developing?*
  - *What particular skills, personal qualities do you think you can contribute?*

  The second list of questions are those that *you* might want at this stage to ask. These questions should link your abilities to your knowledge of the organization and its 'products'. Examples of such questions include:
  - *Would I as a recent graduate be involved in any overseas work?*
  - *Given your current plans for expansion in satellite technology, what further training or personal development opportunities are there likely to be for someone entering at this level?*
- As part of your preparation do look over the CV/application form that you sent off to the organization. Remind yourself of what you've said about yourself. This is particularly important where you have on file a number of possible CVs, see page 116.

> ❏ The interview should be a conversation not an interrogation.

Yes, a conversation. If it does become an interrogation you are most unlikely to be offered the post. Remember the interview has those two important purposes: to help an employer decide on your suitably and to allow you to find a suitable post. It therefore needs to be a conversation.

> ❏ Listen hard all the way through; don't let your attention wander.

As we've said, this interview is supposed to be a conversation so it is important, as in any good conversation, that both sides actually listen to each other. If you don't understand the question then do ask for clarification. Avoid saying: *'I don't understand'* all the time, instead say, *'I'm sorry could you give me an example of that?'*

Don't be tempted to answer *'yes'* and *'no'*. Try and expand on points raised. Remember if you don't put your goods in the shop window so to speak then the buyer can't see!

Avoid this kind of reply to the question:

Q   *'Did you enjoy your course at university?'*
A   *'Yes, most of it, although some parts were a bit boring. But on the whole yes. It was OK.'*

This is too bland, it doesn't give you anything by way of a jumping off point to develop the conversation. It shows you in a poor light, as someone who was rather passive and uninterested in what was going on; someone reactive not proactive.

Activity

How would you have replied to such a question? Think for a while before you read on.

Here's an alternative answer:

A   *'Well, I can't pretend that I enjoyed all the course. Some parts were very much more practical than others so it was much easier to see their relevance to me as an engineer – for instance practical labs, etc. The final year was the most interesting since we had various opportunities to go on placement. Should I say something about that now?'*

Many of you reading this, especially those just finishing their courses will probably think that was rather cheeky but we would call it being assertive. It was a much better answer than the first because it provided a launch pad for further questions, either about the course itself or as we have said, the placements.

Do remember to provide some material for those questions on your personal interests, and so on. To the question:

Q   *'I see volleyball is one of your interests.'*

Avoid saying:

A   *'Yes, I'm very keen on it.'*

Try and provide something a little more by way of flavour and detail. This will allow a conversation to develop through which something about you as a personality will emerge. For example:

> *'Yes, I'm very keen on it. I've played since school days and while at university got involved in some local competitions. We never actually got to the finals of any of these but it was great fun going round seeing other students' sports halls and bars!'*

- Look at your questioner(s). Maintaining good eye contact is often regarded as a sign of openness and confidence on the candidate's part. It also provides you with some indication as to how your answers are being received. If you are faced by a panel then do try and look at the member of the panel who has actually asked you the question, but after a moment do look to the others and engage them in your answer. Remember it will be the whole panel who will be making up their minds about you, not just the one individual, and there's no guarantee that the most influential person will be the one sitting right in front. He or she is more likely than not to be at the side. Avoid looking for too long at one member of the panel who looks more pleasant, attentive, approving (or more attractive) than the others. You need to keep in contact with *all* members of the panel, especially those who might display a negative attitude.

Your voice tone and manner

In our section on presentation, pages 65–81, we cover many aspects of voice use so we won't repeat them, but as a checklist here are some do's and don'ts:

- tone – not too level otherwise you may come across as bored, apathetic, not committed
- stress the key words and phrases if you want others to share your enthusiasm and commitment – inject some stress on what you think is important

- level – you must be heard by all the panel, so strictly no mumbling. This is again where eye contact can be so useful; if you should see the tell-tale signs of your not being heard, for instance people starting to lean forward, their heads bent to one side as if to better catch what you are saying, then do speak up.

Body language

You will find much of this covered in the section of presentation (pages 65–81) but try not to:

- Distract by fidgeting.
- Sit frozen like a rabbit caught in the glare of the headlights; do feel free to move in order to help you relax (remember that it is supposed to be a conversation – don't sit stock still all through!).
- Remember when you sit down that the previous candidate may well have been several inches taller/shorter than you so don't sit down, get comfortable, if the chair is too near the edge of the table, move it away. There's no sense is sitting for half an hour or more and constantly finding yourself banging your legs on the table's edge.
- Don't slouch, maintain an upright, but not a stiff and un-natural posture. Remember it should be a conversation and in any good conversation you would normally shift your posture; you certainly wouldn't sit stiff and unnatural for over 20 minutes!

Dress

The crucial point here is to wear something that makes you feel confident. Don't put on a special interview suit that you only wear for interviews: it will looked stiff and make you look 'odd'. You don't want to come over as awkward. So wear something that fits well. There's no great benefit for you in having to constantly pull at a collar or pull down cuffs or at that tight waistline on trousers or skirt.

Respect convention – suit, collar and tie for men, suit, smart blouse and jacket for women – unless you feel happier and more confident in something less conventional. But do avoid going out to shock. You want the panel to be attending to what you say and not to be spending the first five minutes figuring out what it is you're wearing, being blinded by your tie or jewellery (and that's just the men!).

Questions

Do remember it's a conversation not an interrogation. So do ask questions and don't feel that you have to wait right to the end of the interview before you ask them. The danger if you wait that long is that you will have forgotten what it was you wanted to ask!

At the start of the interviewer the chair of the panel will normally set out the 'groundrules' and suggest that although you will be given time to ask questions at the end of the interview, you will be welcome to ask at any time if you don't understand or if there is a point to make.

What kind of questions should you ask? Do try to make them 'genuine' – i.e. the ones you want to ask not 'special' or 'fake' ones that you've rehearsed for days. Don't ask questions on aspects which have already been covered in the letters and background information already sent to you. If you do it will not impress the panel that you are alert and on the ball.

If you ask questions concerning salary and holidays – do make sure that these haven't already been covered in the background information you were sent. There may well be questions you will need to ask about training and career developments and possibilities for movement around the company if it is large one. Do remember that you really don't have to wait until the end of the interview. It is so important for you to check as the session proceeds that you do understand the questions and their implication. Remember if you don't ask, you don't get!

In some interviews, panels have a way of asking hypothetical questions:

'What would you do if ...?' 'What would your reaction be to ...?'

Obviously it is vital that you check exactly what the questioner is after. Use clarification questions such as:

- *'Do you mean here that the parties would have ...?'*
- *'In this situation would I normally have ...?'*
- *'I take it that much of the preliminary work would have been done before ...'*

In other words what you are doing is to negotiate the boundaries to their probes; that is much better than merely shooting off in the dark.

'Well I'd firstly make sure that ... then ... em ...'

If you jump right in you may have to stop in full flow to check out the preliminaries:

'Oh, by the way would I have had to ...?'

If you have to stop and ask what the boundaries of the question are when you are in fact in the middle of answering then it's not likely that you will make a very good impression on your listeners. It would not reveal you as an attentive would-be professional engineer.

Plugging any gaps

Everyone has some kind of gap in his or her application, a lack of suitable qualifications or experience. As you listen carefully to the questions try and sense from which direction they come from as regards any apparent gaps that the panel may think you have. If you sense this happening then you must do your best to 'plug' this gap by providing some examples, instances to strengthen your case. Remember if you don't do any plugging of these gaps in the interview then it may well be too late and your application will have fallen. You could be assertive and say towards the end of the interview:

'I'm aware that you've asked me a number of questions relating to [whatever the specific deficit].'
'Can I say at this point that I am fully committed to taking further qualifications in ... [or whatever the specification might be].'

Again this might sound a little cheeky to some of you reading this but such a comment will show that you are confident and alert. You may, by doing this, be able to plug a gap which would otherwise undermine your chances. However, even if you do spot the gaps that the panel are aware of and follow this advice to plug them you may still be unsuccessful. You may still not be selected for very good reasons. These may include:

• not enough experience – you're keen but they are looking for someone who can be up and running from day one
• too limited in your qualifications, skills, etc. – they are looking for someone more 'all round', etc.
• not the appropriate personality to fit in with existing team – you are just 'too different' in some kind of way
• they have someone in the organization who is being groomed for the job but they were forced to advertise it.

Apart from this list there are all kinds of other reason for your rejection. Many organizations will offer you feedback on your failure. It is well worth your while taking advantage of this. Your failure may well be for one of the factors in the above list – there may not be much you can do in the short term about these. On the other hand there may be something that you can do to alter your application, a weakness in the way you answered some key questions, a failure to supply some crucial information (i.e. you didn't pick up their cues) or some other aspect of your performance that can be amended in the short term, i.e. before your next interview.

Apart from getting this feedback from the organization after your interview find somewhere quiet to sit down and spend a few minutes thinking through what has just happened – rewind the 'tapes' so to speak and think back on those questions. You might like to jot the ideas down before they disappear from your memory. Consider how you answered their questions. Ask yourself how you reacted to the situations they posed.

- did you provide examples to support any general comments you made?
- were there any particularly awkward questions for which you could have prepared more fully?
- were there any parts of your CV that might have been amplified to show yourself in a more positive light?

This kind of self-appraisal can be very useful. If you don't give it to yourself, who will?

Activity

Think back to an interview you attended in which you were not successful. Ask yourself: How could I have done better? What have I learnt from this experience? What could I do differently next time?

In some selection interviews you will be asked to complete a test. These are often of the paper and pencil variety and are there to assess your team working ability, aspects of your mental aptitudes, etc. The important point is to answer the questions in as honest a way as possible. These tests are very sophisticated, don't try and fake an answer so as to make yours appear 'better' in some way. You will be found out.

Every so often some new craze appears when it comes to selection interviewing. Some years ago the author was in the middle of an interview for the Bank of America in Los Angeles when one of the panel came up and felt the back of his head – phrenology, or analysing the bumps at the back of the head (i.e. to calculate your brain power!) was all the rage. Recently some companies have brought in the services of a graphologist to analyse handwriting and by so doing determine whether the candidate has 'leadership potential'. The lesson is: make sure that your hand-written letter placed alongside your CV is both legible and full of bold brave strokes of the pen and start counting your bumps!

Other interviews

Engineers will frequently have to interview clients, suppliers, other engineers in order to elicit information from them, to gauge their reaction to suggestions, to probe their experience with some innovation, etc.

As with all interviews preparation is essential. Do check out what it is you are expected to do or you want to achieve. (Check with the interviewees what they think the interview will be about.) This assumes that they know that you will be interviewing them. It is often a useful thing for both parties

if the interviewer sends a list of possible questions and areas to be covered in the interview to the other party. This will allow the interviewee to prepare, collect materials and do any necessary 'research' in order to provide a fuller interview.

When interviewing someone do make sure that you arrive in good time and explain the reasons for the interview – even if you have made this clear beforehand – people have short memories. Introduce yourself and explain where you are from – in other words what is your interest in this interview. It is also sensible to outline any 'groundrules' of this interview such as confidentiality, who will get the information and where it will 'end up' in terms of a report, etc. Do remember to have with you and show on request proof of your identity.

Try and maintain eye contact with your interviewee. You will need a list of questions but keep in eye contact. As for recording the information you have various options:

- Take in a tape recorder (you will need to gain permission from the interviewee, you can't just plonk the machine down and assume the other party will be pleased!). Remember too that it is all very well taking in the machine and getting miles of tape recorded but you will then have to transcribe all that tape into text. This can present you with a huge amount of work unless you can audio type or have someone who can do this for you.
- Take in a notepad and make notes as the interview proceeds. There are some techniques used here (for further information on note taking see page 129).
- Do please supply a summary of the main points that he or she has given you. This way you may trigger off further ideas, examples, etc.
- At the end of the interview always ask the interviewee if there are any other points or suggestions he or she would wish to give. In order to prompt these you can supply a short summary of what you think have been the main issues which have emerged. Here is a way that the interviewer doing a communication audit closed his interview:
  - *'To sum up: you feel in general happy with the present state of communication from managers to staff but wish there was more information on changes to the organizational structure?'*
  - *'Are there any additional points you would wish to raise before we close?'*
- If it is a very complicated interview when you have written up your notes it may be useful to phone the interviewee and check whether he or she is happy with the result or has in the interim thought of more details for you to include. Alternatively, you could fax your notes, label them *draft* only, and ask the interviewee to look over them to see if they provide a reasonable record of what passed. We would only recommend this approach if the interview has been very complex. If you keep going back by phone or fax after all your interviews you will quickly lose credibility as an interviewer as well as making a great deal of unnecessary work for yourself.

- When you are eliciting information you are trying to do just this and so avoid letting too many of your own ideas or prejudices creep in. Great care is needed when you are in the writing up stage that you don't bend or angle the words of the interviewee in a way that better fits in with your own notions.

Summary

- Selection interviews are held to find the best candidate for the vacancy and for the candidates to test out if they really want the job. It is in the interests of both parties that both sides of this 'equation' are positive.
- Preparation before the interview is essential. Establish all you can by way of background information on the organization you wish to join. Remember what you have written about yourself in the CV or application form and be prepared to justify it.
- Aim to turn the interview from an interrogation into a conversation.
- It is important during the interview to attempt to 'plug' any gaps that are discovered.
- When carrying out market survey interviews negotiate the groundrules with the interviewee and explain the purpose.
- It is always important to sum up after the interview and to allow the interviewee to add any further thoughts.
- Always write up notes of the interview as soon as possible afterwards.
- Take care to keep your own views and opinions to one side when you carry out a survey or audit. Remain neutral and objective.

Further reading

G Burton and R Dimbleby (1995) *Between Ourselves*. Arnold.
R Ellis and A McClintock (1994) *If You Take My Meaning*, 2nd edition. Arnold.
C Fletcher (1986) *Face the Interview*. Unwin Paperback.
C T Goodworth (1985) *Effective Interviewing*. Business Books.

6

The telephone

In this chapter we outline some key techniques for using the telephone, some tips on making and receiving calls and suggestions as to handling the angry caller.

Introduction

One of the difficulties in writing this chapter is the undoubted fact that almost every one of you is going to mutter under his or he breath: *'Well what's the point of this. I know all about it – I've been using the phone since I was a kid'*.

The point is that the use of the phone is a very important part of being an engineer. We saw in the previous chapter that it is increasingly being used by organizations as part of their selection process. The increasing use of mobile phones means that more and more people will be making use of the phone in all kinds of situations and environments to make contact with colleagues, clients, potential customers, and so on.

Activity

What are your key dislikes when people phone you? Could you jot down a few before you read our list.

- The phone rings and rings – it's a ghost place, no human beings inhabit it.
- They leave you hanging while they pass you on to someone else – or else completely forget about you.
- They get your name wrong.
- Your call is muddled up.
- They snatch up the phone and bark at you.
- They take the details of your message but it is obvious that they are not writing things down since there's no checking back on the spelling of your name, the details of your fax number or the times of the appointment.
- They do answer you but you are aware from the other more pressing conversations in the background (who is going out with whom!); your call is merely an interruption to the social scene in the office!

Are you certain that you don't commit any of these 'crimes'?

Here are some practical tips for more effective telephoning.

Making calls

- Make certain you know why you are making the call. If you're in doubt then it's more than likely that the call will be muddled.
- Resist that temptation to just pick up the phone. Think the call through. If it's an important one, then do make as certain as you can that you won't be interrupted. Turn off that laser printer at your side which may emit white noise over the phone down the line.
- Jot down a short agenda of the points you wish to raise with the other party. There's nothing more frustrating than having completed your call you suddenly remember a key point – some essential detail that you left out – and then you have to phone back!
- When the other party answers the phone it is quite a good idea to just check with him or her that it is a convenient time to call. This is a piece of negotiation that we examined on pages 32–33; it allows the other party to call you back when they are 'more comfortable' – i.e. not in the middle of something, or just about to rush out, or in the middle of eating a sandwich.

We saw in the section on listening (page 35) that it is much easier to listen with your full attention when you haven't got one 'ear' on something else happening.

- If you do listen carefully you should be able to detect if the other party is not very comfortable in taking your call, there will those tell tale signs in the voice – the extra long pauses:

  'well, ...'

  'fine ... yes ... no bother.' (Said with a rising intonation which decoded could mean, 'I am rather busy'!)

  If you have a very talkative party on the other end think up some convincing stratagem to bring things to an end.

  'Sorry but can I bring this to a close, I've got to get to the bar in five minutes.'
- Provide a brief summary of the key points of the call and the action to be taken – do this before you sign off. Make sure that you are certain as to what you are expected to do. The advent of the fax machine has enabled us to make rapid confirmation of the points made in a call. This can be very helpful to both parties; our memories of what was actually said, as opposed to what we think was said, can be very fallible.
- If you are worried by your phone bills, especially the mobile variety, then get a watch with a second by second timer, start it running when you begin your call. You'll soon find out how the minutes go! Your three minutes will soon be up.

- If you are at all nervous about making a call then run it through with someone role playing the other part. This is particularly useful when it comes to that all important phone call to the company who are advertising that so interesting and desirable job!
- Try making your calls in blocks – this way you will find you will get better at them compared to having them spread out through the day. Try and schedule half an hour and make a run of calls. You should notice that you will gain in speed and confidence. This is a good principle of effective time management.

Taking messages

Get into the habit of committing your messages to a message pad. Little scraps of paper not only look untidy about the place but have a habit of not looking important and consequently being buried under piles of other papers.

- If it is not possible for you to write directly on the pad then jot the matter down on a piece of paper – have some scrap on the desk – and then as soon as possible, like now, transcribe it on to the message pad; this should mean that you don't forget any important detail. Here is an example of a simple but effective message pad with original notes above.

Original notes

```
Jim Smith of Hunters Eng called. Please phone him by
11 am tomorr - confirm Paris exhib. He has costings &
will fax these before 5pm - you can see them before
you call him bk.
```

```
Message URGENT   Date April 2nd   Time 11.45 pm
Caller Jim Smith
Organization Hunters Engineering
Their tel number 0181 225-2366 Ext 578
fax number 0181 223-3345
```

Message
```
Please phone Jim Smith by 10am tomorrow April 3rd to
confirm arrangements for Paris exhibition. He has
costings for stands and will fax these to you this pm
(before 5pm) so that you can have a good look at them
before making your call.

Received by   Janet Simpson Ext 51
```

Receiving calls

When you are working in a busy engineering office you will have to take calls which are not for you. As soon as you lift the receiver you are in fact acting as representative for that organization whether it be a firm or your university department or lab. Receiving calls is a responsibility. As you handle that incoming call you are the ambassador of the organization. No matter how brilliant the design and the quality of the engineering, much will depend as far as the credibility of the organization is concerned on how you answer that call.

Avoid just passing callers off into deep space. Check to see if there is actually anyone at that extension.

Here are some points to watch:

- If you don't know the answer to a question, say so – don't be tempted to flounder, avoid this:
  - *'I think Mr Smith's in the building'*
  - *'Yes I'm sure he'll be able to get back to you'* (Oh no he won't, at that moment he's on a plane to Belfast.)

  It's much better to say. *'Please wait one moment and I'll check'*, or even better *'I'm not sure he is in the building, I'll check and if he's not in I'll phone you right back. Can I have your number?'*
- Do speak clearly. Start slowly, remember that the listener will have to tune in to your way of speaking. This is particularly true if you have a marked regional accent. Do remember also that what is to you a pleasant piece of background music may just mean that the caller is robbed of communication with you.
- Do check carefully on details. Watch out for the spelling of names.

Activity

Examine this message and underline those aspects which could be ambiguous/difficult to the reader.

Mr White of Dixons Print left a message for Mr Stevens re: stationery. Could he have usual order for packs by of 10 1st of the month otherwise discounts might have to be 10% higher.

- White or Whyte?
- Dixons Dicksons?
- Mr Stevens/Stephens?
- Usual order?
- 1st of which month?
- What discounts?
- All prices or just those relating to packs?
- Packs of what?

That's rather an extreme situation but you can imagine what problems can be created just because someone failed to check the spelling of a name or the exact number required in the order. The ill-fated charge of the Light Brigade down the wrong valley in the Crimea – the valley with all the Russian guns pointing down it – was caused by a simple error in passing a message. What ill-fated charges, metaphorically speaking, have been caused by one engineer failing to check the telephone message of a colleague?

> Recently a barge went crashing into a bridge in Glasgow. Apparently someone had forgotten to calculate that the materials in the barge would be that much higher when in the barge (because of the flooring) than when on the ground. It might be that in tracking such an error it could have come down to a simple failure to check what one engineer was saying to another. One engineer might not have been active enough in checking for details.

ENGINEER A *'So it'll be 8.76 metres high.'*
ENGINEER B *'That's its total height.'*
ENGINEER A *'Yes 8.76.'*
ENGINEER B *'Is that measured from within the barge?'*
ENGINEER A *'No, good point, that's when its upright on the ground.'*
ENGINEER B *'We'd better know the total height when it's placed in the barge. It could just be important given the height of that bridge and likely clearance.'*

Dealing with difficult callers

Activity

Never allow an angry person on the other end of the line make you lose your temper or be rude in return.

Once you lose your temper the situation is irretrievable. Try and calm the annoyed caller.

> *'I realize this is a nuisance, but if you give me the details I'll make sure that ... and we'll get back to you.'*

Be very careful that in the heat of the moment you don't commit that cardinal sin: over promising and not able to fulfil that promise. Here's an example:

> *'Oh yes, I realize that must have been annoying but I'll ask Mr Johnson to get back to you before your meeting at 11.'*

Oh yes! How do you know that (a) Mr Johnson is in and (b) that he will have the necessary information at his fingertips to make that call by 11 am?

You could become very unpopular by making that kind of call. The temptation to placate that angry 'wasp' on the phone is immense, but don't over promise. A wasp that feels trapped will sting even harder! Once you show some sympathy to the caller's problem and appear to stay calm then this will often rub off on the angry caller and can have a soothing effect.

'I realize that mistake must have caused you a great deal of inconvenience. I shall personally check on what happened and get back to you as soon as possible, certainly by Wednesday. Where can I contact you?'

The telephone, at the present audio and still mostly fixed, in the future increasingly video based and mobile, is a very important contributor to improved communication. The difficulty is that we've all got so used to it that seldom do we think it important. We hope we have alerted you to this.

Summary

- Familiarity can breed contempt. The telephone has been around a long time and can easily be taken for granted.
- The telephone is a vital part of our PR, callers will make judgements about our organization – its credibility and standards – by the way we take the calls.
- We should learn from those calls which were handled badly.
- We may need to negotiate the most appropriate time to make a call.
- We should prepare a brief agenda for calls so that we don't miss key points.
- Because of the speed at which our memory of a call fades we need to keep accurate notes in a log to remind us of the key points.
- We need to be very careful when acting for others that we don't 'over promise' and then have to retract.
- We need as recipients to check very carefully spellings of names, details of dates, exact numbers, etc. We mustn't put down the receiver and still be bemused. We need to be active listeners on the phone.
- In dealing with difficult callers we need to try and separate out the anger or awkwardness from the person making the call and the actual problem.

Further reading

D Rowntree (1988) *The Manager's Book of Checklists*. Corgi.
R Holden (1988) *Stress Busters: 101 recipes for stress survival*. Thorsons.

Part III

7

Communication to groups

We examine the various stages that groups may have to go through before they can function effectively. We look at the concept of team types, the dangers of groupthink and the dangers of compliance, plus the effects on the group of the environment and culture in which they operate.

Introduction

Now we've arrived at communication with groups and moved away from one-to-one communication. Many of the principles of communication will be similar for both.

By groups we mean anything from a few people to an audience of 50 plus. As we did with one-to-one communication let us take note of the various factors which mark out this form of 'bridging the gap'.

- Because we are working with a group it is often more difficult to work out the attitudes, expectations and motivations of its members. In a one-to-one communication, although it may be difficult, it is usually easier to get 'inside' the other person and tease out what makes him or her 'tick'. It is usually easier to 'read' the non-verbal elements on a one-to-one basis compared to being faced with a number of people with their varying attitudes and expectations. There is also the fact that normally we are further away from them than would be the case when communicating with one other. We have already seen something of the problems of this at panel interviews. We certainly can try hard to decode the non-verbal behaviours of all those sitting in front of us, but it is difficult.
- There is the plain fact that there is more communication – verbal and non-verbal – coming at you from a group than from a single person. There is more energy required of you as a communicator. This is an important fact when it comes to the preparation of material for communicating to a group. Whereas in a one-to-one situation we can (but it is not recommended) muddle through a communication hoping to negotiate and find some compromise, this is very risky with a group unless you have someone in the group who can act as spokesperson; this means that we are in fact negotiating with one person.

- There is a greater risk of failure with a group communication. This is particularly true when making any kind of presentation – here the risk is so apparent – all those expectant faces turned up looking at you! The risk element is also there, but not so dramatic when you send out a report or memo or letter; these may be addressed to the one person but solo directed communications have a habit of leaking to others.

We hope that all this is not putting you off from communicating with groups. There are some advantages:

- It may often be easier to obtain feedback from a group rather than the one person. This is obvious when you think of it. If after you've carried out a one-to-one communication you then ask for some kind of feedback on your performance it may be very difficult for that other person to provide you with that kind of criticism. You know how it is – you're sitting with that other person and then he or she asks you: *'Well how did that go?'* and then you say, *'Well it was OK'*. Now that is a great deal of help, as you can appreciate!

With the group when you ask them for any kind of feedback it is a little easier since each member can as it were 'hide' in the anonymity of the membership. This is particularly true if the group is divided into subgroups and each of these is asked its opinion.

- The second advantage is that it is a much more efficient way of communicating, rather as lectures are an efficient way of getting information to large numbers of students at one sitting. Notice we are saying efficient, we are not making any judgements about effective – that is something else. We examined notions of effectiveness and efficiency of communication on pages 8–9.

The stages groups should go through

As we did for one-to-one communication we'd like to provide a very brief 'helicopter' view of some of the principal theories relating to group communication. We supply you with some reading at the end of this section if you'd like to pursue this area.

Researchers have been drawn to the question: *'Why is it that some groups appear to work more successfully that others whether they be sporting teams, Polar explorers, Army units or British Cabinets?'*

Tuchman in 1968 came up with the valuable notion that all groups had a number of stages that they should pass thorough. In summary he called these:

- *Forming*: that is when the group comes together, gives itself a name and starts to finds its feet.

- *Storming*: this is the time when groundrules get settled, ways of conducting business are sorted out, constitutions may be amended, and so on.

According to Tuchman this is a very valuable time. It is when things should get aired, issues discussed openly, conflict which might later infect the group is dealt with. (We will see a method of doing this on page 90.)

Tuchman says that those groups who do *not* go through this conflict stage, these storms, may experience very real and lasting tensions later in working together. They may in fact get stuck.

- *Norming*: this is when the group has settled and has developed some 'norms' for itself – ways of procedure which most members will be happy about.
- *Performing*: the group is working with most if not all individuals understanding their roles within it. It is working smoothly and getting things done.
- *Adjourning or Death*: the group's work is completed. It decides to fold. There are rather too many groups that should have 'died' but stick grimly on. Perhaps you have experienced the kind of thinking:

> 'It's Tuesday afternoon; time for our Tuesday group. We always meet on Tuesday. Tuesday afternoon – a regular slot in my diary for the meeting. Why? How need you ask. Because it's Tuesday and we always have meetings on Tuesday. Besides there's tea and biscuits – chocolate ones too! I never miss Tuesday meetings.'

Activity

Have you experienced being a member of a group which got stuck using the Tuchman terminology. Why was this? Did you manage to get it unstuck?

Team types

Belbin has spent a great deal of his life researching this question: 'Why do groups fail despite having a clear goal and effective leadership?' He isolated the fact that successful groups require a mix of types or personalities to perform well. We thoroughly recommend his own books on this work. Here is a brief summary of his findings.

In a group we provide two roles: we have our *technical* role, that is our engineering skills and experience, the other is what we are, our personalities and the way we think and react. We bring to the group something special because we are what we are. This is our *team* role. He isolates some eight of these types. You may have used his self-analysis test to discover which is your preferred team type or types. You may well be given a form of this test as part of a selection interview.

The danger he suggests from his extensive research is that where groups are limited to only a few of these personality types or where they are deficient in a particularly important one, then the group will underperform and may be seriously weakened.

For instance, one of his team types is called the 'Shaper'. The characteristics of this type is that he or she is outgoing, dynamic, full of drive and readiness to challenge. The down side of this (the allowable weakness as Belbin puts it) is a tendency to impatience and irritation at delay. You can imagine what would happen if you had a team full of these types. You would get a great deal of heat and struggle but would you get good decisions? Would you have well-led meetings? It would be like taking a number of cats for a walk.

What can we do then if we are in a group where some of these roles are not present? Belbin suggests that we should seek to import them to make the group richer. We may find that because our business at meetings never seems to be getting anywhere we need to bring in a Shaper to help move things along a bit faster.

Secondly, under good positive and open leadership members of the group will be more likely to show their true selves rather than hide behind a fiction. One of his types is the Plant, so called because Belbin suggests that many teams have to actively import such a person. They are characteristically imaginative, full of good ideas, bright, creative; their allowable weakness is that they may have their heads in the clouds and not be very attentive when the group is in the middle of some discussion. The problem for Plants is that if you have a leader or chairperson who is very much a Shaper and wants to proceed the business as fast as possible then Plant-type thinking may not be allowed to flourish. In this case the Plant will keep his or her characteristics from emerging for fear of being told off or hurried up.

'Not another of your crazy ideas surely? Come on we must make a decision!'

You can imagine the value of such a person in an engineering context, someone with the ability to see a problem in a different light. There are accounts of the early days of NASA and the race to the Moon where Plant-like thinking enabled brilliant short cuts to be made to the moon landing plan. (*'You can't bring the rocket back, what you need is to use it as a launch vehicle for a small pod – remember the reduced* gravity *effects on the moon'*). This kind of creative thinking gave rise to the Eagle landing and relaunch system which functioned so brilliantly in the July 1969 landing on the Moon.

So when you are in a group that does not seem to be getting very far consider whether you need to import a Plant to stir you up with some creative thinking. (For a further discussion on this, including mention of De Bono's six hats, see page 73.)

Belbin has listed other types: the Completer Finisher – one who is very strong on finishing or seeing that all the loose ends are tied up but who can be rather a worrier over small things. The Monitor Evaluator, one who is good at asking the important questions: Why? How? How much? Then there is the Chairman, a person who acts calmly, gets people to talk, is good at drawing out the key points and is a good listener. One who in fact makes a good chair.

Activity

Before you read on think of the various groups of which you have been a member. What personality types have you brought to these? Have you been more a Plant than a Shaper, or more of Completer Finisher than Monitor Evaluator? Which is your preferred role?

Groupthink

The other researcher we would like to commend to you is Janis, an American who has studied what he calls Groupthink. He defines this as:

> 'What happens when a group of people who respect each others' opinions arrives at a unanimous view, each member is likely to feel that the belief must be true. This reliance on consensus validation tends to replace individual critical thinking'.

This tendency not to 'rock the boat' resembles what Tuchman calls a lack of a storming stage. You may have been in a group where this Groupthink happened. The group gets very cosy and no one wants to say what he or she feels for fear of upsetting the others and being a 'bad sport'. In engineering this could have very serious consequences. Accounts of engineering disasters such as at the nuclear station at Three Mile Island seem to suggest that some engineers in the team were worried at the procedures being used but did not speak up for fear of seeming to be disloyal to their mates. The longer the group works together the more difficult it often is to step out of line and be critical. This is why it is a good idea to have the occasional 'spring' clean – a team review so that grievances can be aired before they build up to become real explosions. (See page 90 for examples of this review.)

Conformity pressures

Closely allied to this problem is one where the dominating influence of the leader or chairperson actually reduces any tendency to give vent to criticism. This is where conformity of view on the surface masks a great deal of hidden anxiety underneath. Recently published memoirs of serving ministers in the Thatcher and Wilson administrations suggest that this happened on a number of occasions. On the surface all seemed to support a proposal but in the corridors few appeared to be in favour. The fear of losing one's job or influence in the team may account for much of this loss of nerve.

These then are just some of the theoretical aspects that make group communication so fascinating. There are a number of other issues in group formation and development; these include:

The tendency for groups to make risky decisions

There has been a good deal of study as to this phenomenon. It appears that whereas an individual may have to consider how the decision will rebound on him or her personally when that person is a member of a group, there is some measure of anonymity. In other words it is the group that is making the decision not Harry or Susan as individuals. This is reinforced where the minutes or notes of the group's decisions are recorded without the inclusion of names. *It was decided that ...* rather than *Harry Smith's recommendations were agreed to.*

It is important therefore that as members of a group we should, while wishing to be a full member of the group, keep a weather eye open for those decisions that are 'risky' and make sure that someone in the group acts as a Monitor Evaluator (another Belbin type) and asks some searching questions:

- *Will it work?*
- *What will be the likely consequences?*
- *How do we know our decision will work?*
- *What unplanned effects may occur as a result of our decision?*

The effect of the situation and the environment

In our discussion of presentation skills in the next chapter we shall see just how important the lack of ventilation in a room can be for a speaker. In our section on meetings (Chapter 9) we examine the effect that the layout of the tables and chairs may have on the success of the communication. We also need to be aware of the context in which our communication with the group is set. For instance, is this the first meeting of the group? If that is the case some introductions and ice breaking may be necessary. Is this group one where morale is low, motivation has sunk out of sight and the leadership is non-existent? If so we may have to refocus its remit, redefine the group composition and review with members of the group just what kind of leadership would be most appropriate.

The effect of different cultures on groups

If you work as an engineer in Japan for instance you need to remember that much group communication – meetings for example – are held to ratify ideas and policy not to discuss and argue a case. This storming stage is most often done behind the scenes and in small informal groups (sometimes in the evenings in a sake bar). To start arguing and disagreeing over policy matters in front of the group, as would be common in Europe and the United States, may well be regarded as bad mannered behaviour in Japan and throughout much of the Far East. Meetings are often ceremonial in form. Tea may be drunk, papers signed and hands shaken, ice breakers that we might feel happy using could impose real embarrassment to a group of Chinese engineers. We need to feel our way slowly in these situations if we wish to avoid causing any offence or embarrassment. We need to be aware of the cultural dynamics, rules and social conventions which govern groups in particular societies. The author has worked in Finland, training managers. The group sessions tend to be hard working and serious, starting at 6 am in the morning and breaking for lunch at 11.30 am. The ice breaking (literally) was done over beer and sausages in the sauna.

In so many social and work situations one has to respect these group norms and conventions. Damage may be done to relationships by behaving in a group in the same way as would be the case at home. Engineers working across borders and time zones may often need to bridge more than just the time gap.

Summary

- Groups represent several distinct challenges to us as communicators: their reactions are often more difficult to assess as are their likely attitudes and expectations. There may well be a greater risk of failure when communicating to them.
- The advantages of working with groups are that it is usually easier to get more reliable feedback than when communicating with individuals.
- Groups appear to need to go through certain distinct stages; if they get stuck they may not perform well.
- We bring to a group team and technical roles. Groups may not perform well because there is not enough variety of team role present.
- Groupthink and conformity can blight many groups; we must be aware of these factors and the risky shift that may occur because we as individuals are to some extent submerged in the group. The responsibility for making a decision may be hidden.
- We need to consider the effect of environment and culture on a group's behaviour and performance.

Further reading

J Adair (1986) *Effective Team Building*. Gower.
M Belbin (1984) *Managing Teams*. Heinemann.
E De Bono (1985) *Six Thinking Hats*. Penguin.
C B Handy (1988) *Team Building*. Kogan Page.

8

Giving a presentation

We provide you with advice on how to cope with nerves, and being positive about yourself as a speaker. We examine methods of audience analysis, preparation of your material, the use of cue notes to assist your delivery, as well as verbal and non-verbal delivery. We suggest various strategies for large audiences as well as smaller more informal ones. Finally we suggest various ways of handling questions.

Introduction

So it's come at last – the time for your ordeal, that presentation you have been asked (requested) to give to your group who you feel won't particularly want to hear it. So why are you giving it, except to satisfy some ritual, some assessment (i.e. as part of some examination or interview), because of some tradition or because your boss/tutor has asked you? People very seldom volunteer to give presentations.

Let's assume that there's no escape; the audience are already primed, advance warning has been given, the room booked! Your credibility is on the line. The only way forward is forward.

> ❏ Being positive about yourself; being enthusiastic about your message is essential in giving a presentation.

This chapter is about how you can become more positive when giving a presentation. If you are not feeling positive about yourself and your material the audience will soon notice.

Being positive – reducing your nerves to manageable proportions

Recently the British Women's Athletic Federation asked an industrial psychologist to see what could be done to improve the morale of the team. She called them together and asked them to say as a team the words: 'we are world beaters'. Only a few murmurs came out, just a trickle of enthusiasm. After some time working with them, getting them to examine their own image and to find what was wrong with it, did they all feel able to shout out: '**we are world beaters**'. As she said, 'if you don't believe in yourselves who else will?'

This is not to suggest that we all need to shout out, *'I'm just a wonderful presenter'*, but there has been enough research done to suggest that having a positive self-image, having a belief in one's self and one's message is crucial to any result, whether that be on the sports field, being interviewed or making a presentation. Engineers, especially in the UK, have perhaps not been as positive about themselves and their message as they might have been! There are many possible reasons for this being the case: lack of public esteem, failure to market themselves aggressively, the structure of their education and training, etc.

So be positive. **Think positive**. There's no more rapid turn off for an audience than hearing the presenter apologize for his or her inadequacies, failures to prepare, lack of time, etc. Avoid these excuses at all costs. Audiences are just not interested. They will reduce your credibility.

Who is your audience?

Let's start by thinking about the audience. One way to manage our nerves is to direct anxiety away from ourselves and towards those who will be listening to us. We need to get the target into our sights. Too many people plan their presentations without doing this essential targeting. Remember that your audience will share a different kind of anxiety – that you are going to be a flop! So consider this:

> ❏ First and foremost the audience will normally start off on your side.

This may appear to be bordering on the incredible but if you think for a moment you'll see that it's true. An audience, any audience, dislikes being embarrassed. It's an awful experience, you don't know where to look with a speaker who is so nervous, so badly prepared, has been so badly briefed, hasn't done any homework on the subject.

Think of those times when you've been in an audience which has ended up squirming because the speaker went on for too long, failed to stay on the topic, patronized or insulted the audience, pitched the level of the material wrongly or failed to amuse them by an inappropriate or stale joke or story.

If you manage to avoid these errors then, on the whole, your audience won't necessarily say 'we love you', but will more likely be on your side than someone who ignores these aspects. There will always be some audiences who despite all you can do for them will not be on your side. What do you think could be the reasons for such a negative attitude? Consider these reasons:

- They've been sitting for too long listening to a previous speaker who drastically over ran on time. (Give them a break before you start.)
- They've already heard much if not all of what you're telling them from a different speaker or source. (Add your angle; keep it short.)
- They've been told to sit there and would far rather be doing something else. (Say what you want to say, be brief and add interesting examples.)
- They know more than you do (make sure you find an angle where you can add some value – your experience, your particular new angle).

Clarify your task

Speakers are often unnecessarily nervous because they are unsure of what is *expected* of them by their audiences. So it is vital that you clarify your remit – the task that the audience expects you to carry out. We shall say more about remits when looking at reports (pages 140–141) and meetings (pages 83–84).

Many presentations cause disappointment because the audience are expecting one thing and they receive another. Do check and double check that you have the necessary information so that you can prepare material at the right level, depth and length. We'll say more about this aspect later in the chapter.

See it this way: a speaker starts off with certain credit in the bank. Let's call it £1000. If he or she fails to follow these 'rules' then by the time he or she has sat down there could only be £500 in the account, even less. I can think of some who would end up penniless! Mind you, if you not only follow these rules but the other advice outlined in this chapter then you may well have more than you started with.

Case study

Examine the following transcript of a presentation given by a recently qualified engineer. He has been asked to make this presentation on an aspect of his work for a competition organized by his local chamber of trade who wish to highlight schemes to improve client care. He has been given 10–15 minutes which will include time for questions.

Here is a transcript of his talk. Think as you read it of where you might give him advice if you were sitting listening to him rehearse it. Say what you would praise; with something so personal as criticism we need to balance the negative with the positive. Naturally the transcript cannot show you all the facial expressions and gestures he would have used but it will give you the flavour.

> Hello. My name is Roger Bolt. My project involved me in looking at some ways to improve customer care in the civil engineering company where I work. It's called Flex and Rivet in the city centre. They were established in ...
>
> I started off by making a review – sort of what we were doing – imagining that the client was approaching our company for the first time. They may have heard about our work or read one of our brochures. They may have seen one of our advertisements in the trade journals.

Comment

The speaker has failed to set his stall out – to clarify his aim. he's already into the 'story' and many of us in the audience are not sure why we're listening.

I surveyed all our printed materials. I put them through a readability check and made some revisions. I've selected one page on this slide. You will be able to see the difference in layout and design of the printed page. What you cannot see from this is the number of long and awkward sentences we've pruned.

Comment

If the audience can't see why bother mentioning it. It only causes frustration.

I then carried out a survey with some of our clients as to how friendly and approachable they had found our reception and office staff. Most of our clients will be phoning us to establish contact so that it is very important that they are greeted in a friendly way. I discovered that none of three reception and office staff have had any customer care training. We arranged some internal training which involved using a recording device to monitor calls and play them back to the receptionists with the help of an outside facilitator. This training seems to have resulted in a more friendly telephone manner.

Comment

It's often useful when your talk runs through several distinct stages or processes to have a menu slide or flip chart page to indicate the basic structure and to demonstrate your progress.

I then looked at what happens next in the chain. When clients come to the office to discuss their needs I wondered what kind of impression the office environment created. I took photographs – would you like to pass these round.

Comment

Not to be recommended! As you pass things round so it causes a distraction. Wait until the end.

You can see that the signage is rather cluttered and that the reception desk itself is not very well positioned. In discussion with the manager, my boss, and also my placement manager. I decided to make some improvements to this area. The next set of photos shows some of the changes. You can see – sorry I'd better wait until you've all had a chance. Yes?

Comment

You should at the outset set the groundrules as far as taking questions is concerned. If you are thrown one like this you may be put right off your stride. Be assertive and say that there will be time for questions later.

Did the manager agree with you in making these changes?

Yes, he was enthusiastic. Yes.

Had there been much done on other aspects of client care before you started?

Well, the manager had only recently taken over, so I'm not certain what had happened before. You've all seen the photo, you can see then that the reception area was too hidden and there was too much clutter around – the entrance needs to be made more up-market to reflect the desired image.

Was there any resistance from the regular staff

Jim, I'll come to that in a minute, but thanks ... One of the main problems I had was getting the lighting in the entrance improved. You can see – well sorry I must have forgotten the chart – well take my word for it – the old lighting was very bright and glaring – it certainly didn't fit in with the image we were trying to create – more up market and expensive lighting displays. Here are some – I'll just sketch these on the board here.

Comment

Not a bad idea to have a flip chart of board handy so that you can do the quick sketch, write up a name, etc. Do make sure that there is a pen (that works) and that you draw the shape or the letters big enough. It's a good idea to do a little practising beforehand!

You can see what potential there was; just look at this for instance, this could be fitted in ... [*he continues to describe drawbacks of the various fixtures, fittings, designs; this goes on for 2–3 minutes; he now has only five minutes left*].
   I seem to have spent rather too much time on this reception area.

Comment

Yes he has. This is such a danger. Do keep your eye firmly on the clock. Don't be tempted to stray. Stick to time!

Others aspects of client care included the way we handle contracts, the follow up we give to clients after having signed contracts and many other aspects of client or customer care. Well, I seem to be running out of time.
   Well, I'll have to stop there, here have been some of the changes that I was able to make at my placement to improve client care. So, I think it's vital that engineering firms present an up-to-date and professional image to their clients. I mean if the retail and

service sector can do it why not engineering? It's all very well having excellent skills and marvellous designs but one has to sell these in a very competitive marketplace. Now if you have any questions ...

Comment

A very rushed conclusion. Key points left out in the scramble to finish. What a wasted opportunity. A strong conclusion is one way to hammer your message home and stimulate questions. The more active involvement there is the more you can 'hook' your audience.

To summarize the deficits in this presentation:

- There was insufficient attention given to the preparation of this talk.
- The structure was rather difficult to follow.
- The time keeping was poor; the speaker spent far too much time on one aspect (the office design) and subsequently had to rush important aspects of contract management.
- He got into a muddle over the way he answered the questions.

Activity

Here is a possible revision. Read it carefully and consider what improvements have been made and where you might suggest additional ones.

Good evening. My name is Roger Bolt My project involved me in looking at some methods to develop client care in the firm where I work. This is Flex and Rivet. It is a well established civil engineering company ...

The aim of this short talk is to highlight some aspects of client care. You may think this perhaps an unusual topic for a newly qualified engineer to select but I feel that it is a very important part of running a successful engineering company. It also allowed me to examine aspects of design and current office systems and their management. Customer care is central to the engineering industry. We depend on our customers and their coming back.

Comment

Useful introduction: sets the scene briefly and provides a much clear aim than version one.

I started off by making a review of how we initially communicate with our clients – our printed brochures, advertisements and general publicity material. I subjected our brochures, etc. to a readability and design survey. I don't have time now to go into details on this but if you are interested in the system we used I can discuss this after the presentation.

> ## Comment
> Very wise. This is being assertive and polite.

Basically I discovered that too much of our brochure material was difficult to read, and there were several rather ambitious expressions. I've selected a few of these on this slide. As you can see it's not very easy to see quite what we mean here. Would anyone like to make an offer? Yes ... Well, I don't think that's what the company meant. And that really does illustrate my point. If you read that way and the company this way then that's not a very good beginning to a business relationship.

> ## Comment
> An interesting idea to involve the audience. You have to watch that you don't get side-tracked.

I then examined how when clients have decided to contact us we actually welcome their business. I started with the way we answer any telephone requests. I carried out an informal survey with some of existing clients – again if you'd like details on this I'd be more than happy to supply them. What emerged was that although our reception staff seemed on the ball and were efficient at answering questions and putting clients to the engineers, we might sound a little more happy and welcoming. As a result of this feedback I carried out short in-house coaching courses with the help of an outside trainer. This involved the recording and playing back to analyse the results of a number of typical calls. All we engineers in the office have noticed an improvement in terms of friendliness of manner from reception staff.

> ## Comment
> The structure and sense of progress is much better than in version one.

[*He goes on to describe his actions in some detail.*]
I took these photos before we made any changes. I hope you will be able to come up and look at them when I've finished. Can I complete this section and then I'll be happy to take questions.

> ## Comment
> It is much more sensible to pass round photos after the talk. Notice how he is being assertive with questioners.

One of the improvements I wanted to carry out – and in this [*He continues with this part of the talk, outlining the various plans for change*]. I've given you some information on what I tried to do to improve one firm's client care. I hope you'll come up and have a look at the photographs. As I said at the start, engineering is very much a service industry as any other – we have our customers. I suggest that in the past we haven't taken on board customer care in the way that other commercial organizations have done. We have assumed that clients will come because of the excellence of our engineering work and our reputation for getting things done. In part this is as true as ever it was. However, we must not neglect those aspects of our offices – the way in which we communicate with our clients. I hope this talk has stimulated plenty of thought and perhaps some questions. Yes ...

Comment

A much better conclusion. He summarizes the key points of his talk and leads the way nicely into questions from the floor.

This was a better presentation. In particular:

* It does keep to time. The speaker is not forced to hurry through certain sections and then fail to reach a conclusion.
* There is more of a structure: he appears to be keeping to some kind of plan.
* He is more assertive with questioners.

On the other hand there could have been:

* Better linkage between points
* Some indication of *costs*; he is after all working for a business;
* More detail as to the *type of firm*, its clientele and their expectations.

What the first version of the speech illustrates very well is the lack of preparation that went into it. It's time to examine this aspect more closely.

Preparation

There is no avoiding this one. There are a few things in life that one can get by without a lot of preparation, but giving a presentation is not one of them. Remember the key point: who is my audience?

❏ If you haven't thought of what you want to say before you stand up then you are asking for trouble.

Even if you know the material very well and have given the same talk many times before, memory has the nasty habit of going blank on you and your credibility can suffer an alarming drop – your £1000 can soon drop to a mere £500!

Here are some suggested stages in the planning of your talk.

- We suggest you try a brainstorm for a start; this is where you place the topic you've been given, or the one you've selected, in the centre of the page and consider as many as possible different perspectives and angles as you can possibly think of. The point here is that unless you do this it is so easy just to produce the predictable, the obvious and the downright dead boring. This is particularly the case if you have given the talk many times before and you're feeling stale about it.

Suppose as an example that the topic that has been given to you was in your particular field; let's say it was in risk management and the topic computer modelling. A nice general topic; in fact a hopelessly general one. Beware of being invited to talk on such a wide and vague topic. Always try and focus the ideas down to something manageable both for you and your audience.

The whole point about a brainstorm is that it may kick start you into thinking of a good idea, a promising angle. You may have got tramlined into a particular way of thinking about a subject. Take a clean sheet of paper and look at the subject from a completely fresh angle. Put the topic in the centre of the paper and let all the possible ideas spin from this point. The essence of an effective brainstorm is that any idea, no matter how improbable, is permissible. Keep the censor away. Don't discard an idea just because it doesn't appear to fit in with previous notions. It was at a gathering of computer scientists during a brainstorm on future developments that someone said: 'Why always use a keyboard, how about something you can hold in the hand?' A crazy notion perhaps but out of such came the idea of the mouse!

Edward De Bono has a nice idea of 'six hats' to aid the thinking process. He suggests that we need to develop different ways of thinking through a problem, so the 'white' for information getting, 'red' for thinking from emotion, 'black' when you are looking at risk assessment and caution, 'green' for possibilities and 'blue' when you want the overview and 'yellow' for logical positive thinking.

Let's see what a brainstorm on this subject may have produced. Be prepared to don various hats. The topic has now been narrowed down to the 'preparation' stages of risk management. You might like to jot down a few ideas on this topic in a solo brainstorm. See how many ideas you can produce.

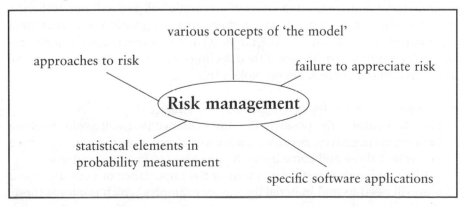

You may have got more on your brainstorm. The important thing is to collect as many ideas as possible. It's so easy simply to accept the usual approach, the usual 'menu' and so get ourselves and our audiences stuck in a rut.

• We now need to do some serious angling and positioning of the material so gathered for our intended audience. I suggest that you put up in bold the following headings on your next sheet of paper.

Audience (checklist)

• Their expectations and likely attitudes to the subject.
• Level expected (i.e. previous knowledge of subject).
• Number expected (how far will I have to project my voice?).
• Context of presentation, i.e. one of several, by itself, part of a series, for an assessment, etc.
• Environment in which presentation is to be given.

Notice that we start with these aspects first, rather as we would with a report, our terms of reference (see page 140). We need to know the kind of audience we are going to have to face. Normally we do have a pretty good idea how many there will be.

Do check on this; it can be a terrible shock, speaking from bitter experience, to walk into a room expecting to give an informal talk to a handful of persons, then the doors open to reveal a lecture theatre full! So don't accept the organizer's vague, *'well it'll be about ...'*, try and find out a little more.

❑ Never accept vagueness from an organizer when it comes to a presentation. Check all the assumptions (see the section on visual aids and room layout, page 187).

But of all the background questions that we should consider and have answers provided, those relating to audience *expectations* and *attitudes* are by far the most important. We talked in Chapter 1 of the importance of angling your material. But we need to know which angle will best suit our audience. It's not a blunderbuss approach we require, just firing various points at them from our brainstorm, but a precise targeting at their expectations, at their attitudes, taking into consideration their feelings, positive, neutral or negative about us and our subject. Let us explain this.

• *Audience favourably disposed to you and your message.*
Look to reinforce the positive. Provide evidence that will avoid dwelling too long on negatives. Because you are in a strong position you can afford to mention these and come up with your ideas to improve matters.
If the audience is fairly convinced of the importance of your argument you will need to find material by way of examples which reinforce these.

You can afford to present the other aspects and since they are positively on your side they will not mind.

- *Neutrally disposed to you/your message.*
  Re-state the importance of your message. Supply facts and carefully selected examples to back up your material.
- *Negative attitude to you/your message.*
  Respect their attitudes, don't criticize. Keep it brief, state your reasons in a calm manner. Find a few powerful and highly credible examples and stick to precise facts. Avoid too much personal opinion. Try and spend time in any intervals, coffee breaks to influence on a one-to-one basis.

Notice that last point. It is often during the question and answer sessions and especially during any short breaks in the proceedings such as over coffee, that you can do more direct influencing.

There is often little that you can do to change deeply set attitudes, but you can do your honest best, lay out the situation as you see it, acknowledge that some of the audience may see things differently but you have been given an opportunity and you intend to say what you believe to be important.

Normally if you are up front in this way with your listeners then most will give you a hearing. Your hope in changing or softening their attitudes will rest on the way you carry your ideas, the facts and examples you bring and, perhaps more importantly, the time spent in one-to-one conversation and persuasion after the presentation. You need to think and plan ahead for your follow-up, and don't rush away at the end. If you do your influence will rapidly fade.

Organization and structuring of your material

We have brainstormed and collected a number of ideas; we have angled the material to suit the attitudes and expectations of our tutor and audience. Now we need to *structure* it for easy understanding. You need to provide 'motorway signs' so that your listeners know where you are taking them and have some indication of your destination. Think of the sandwich: three parts with meat in the middle. Set out your notes as so:

Introduction	Development	Summary/conclusion
Aims in talk	Main points	Brief summary
Reason for speaking	Action points	
Length/width of coverage		

This serves to set out the key ideas and provides you with some definite progress through your subject. Do provide some linkages between the parts. Unless you are going to be quoted by the media or you are giving an academic paper where every word is important, my strong advice is not to read out your speech. This is not to say that it isn't an idea to write out most of what you want to say, but use this as a *base* from which you construct your talk. However, do not lay out your speech notes like this.

```
                       Risk management

Is important in engineering because in order
to design and construct we must be as
certain as possible that we are working to
acceptable levels of risk.
There are few current computer programs to
assist in the complex calculations that are
necessary in risk management. As an example
let us look at the chemical industry.
```

Can you suggest an alternative? Would you prefer:

```
                       Risk management

Mins    Aims: Review RM within industry            Flip Cht
              Provide examples
              Suggest future developm'ts        OHP slide 1
4

        RM within chemical ind.
              More comp'tn = more pressure
              on st'ndrds
              Some companies left b'hind
              - not react'g fast en'gh

8       Example
              Plastic plant. Case study          OHP slide 2
              Poor cal of risk
```

What are the advantages of the second layout?

- For a start it is much less cluttered and will provide the speaker many more opportunities to look up at the audience and share the material with them.
- The visual aids are indicated on the right-hand margin where they are easily noticed – an important point if you are in a bit of a panic!
- Approximate timings are put on the left-hand margin. It's very important for your confidence as a speaker that you know how long you're supposed to speak for. It's a horrible fate to peter out after a few minutes with an expectant audience hoping you'll go on for at least another 20. Equally, it is a poor boost to your confidence to be given warning signs by the

chairman to come to a conclusion just as you are getting into your stride. So do get into the habit of rehearsing your talk out aloud and take a note of the timings.

• The key words and phrases act as triggers: they trigger off the ideas you have been so carefully preparing. However, this arrangement may fill you with horror.

What happens (you may well ask) if the so-called triggers fail and you peer down at the sheet and nothing much happens. Well, this usually reflects the lack of preparation that has been put in.

You have to know the material – we don't mean memorized – but know it sufficiently well for the triggers to be able to work. It also means spending enough time running through the material so that it is fresh in your mind.

> ❏ Making a presentation is very much about building a relationship with your audience. Contact is essential.

If the speaker reads the text then it is very difficult for any relationship to be achieved. The members of the audience may well feel as though the speaker is not that much bothered with them and so their attention may fall away; that is unless the scripted material is so riveting.

Consider the puppeteer controlling the puppet via the strings. Think of your audience. You wish to stay in touch with them. Your ability to look at them and share with them is akin to the puppeteer's strings. If the strings go slack, the eye contact falls away, the influence will diminish and eventually you will have little or no control over your audience. There is also the commonly held perception that if speakers do not look at their audiences then they are either not very confident with their material or have something to hide. This may not be true in your case but it is a widely held perception.

We repeat: this does not mean that you have to memorize the speech, that would be unwise since in the stress of the moment you are likely to forget much of it, and secondly, it makes it all seem very lacking in spontaneity. Notice in the above example, the figures on the left of the notes. These are reminders to you as to your time allocation. In rehearsal as you speak the words aloud you will be able to get some idea of how time is passing; jot this information down. It should give you a little more confidence that either (a) you have enough information or (b) you won't overrun your time limit. Having mentioned the word contact then what kinds of contact should we be thinking of?

Activity

Jot down your own list before you turn over.

You might have included:

- *Vocal contact.*
  Being heard, being audible to the back of the room. When you stand up to speak do try and aim your voice at a particular spot in the room – imagine you are removing a spot of dust somewhere towards the back row. So often a speaker will come up and just continue in the same way, with the same vocal projection as used in conversation with organizer/tutor, etc. This just won't do when there are a crowd of people and perhaps outside noise as well. This is being assertive.
- *Language contact.*
  Using the appropriate level of vocabulary, the appropriate use of jargon (i.e. jargon which the audience will be familiar with). It's no use saying TQM if no one in the audience understands this means total quality management.
- *Visual contact.*
  Your own 'visual' appearance; how you appear to the audience. Will they be put off by the loudness of your tie, the insignia on T-shirt, etc.? Do you look appropriate for the task? Do you feel comfortable?
  The visual aids that you make use of in your presentation (see page 185 for details).
- *Non-verbal contact.*
  This is partly connected with your appearance but includes many more aspects. For instance, do you make unnecessary gestures which may distract your audience? It is very important to start by standing or sitting still so that you do not distract. Then when you have gained the audience's attention you can act in a natural way with your usual gestures. Many people who watch their presentations on video become very self-conscious about any gestures that they make; what they tend to forget is that the camera is usually showing close up and that in a real presentation the audience may be several metres away – the gestures just blend into the background, that is unless they are very exaggerated. In our experience there are very few people who use too many or too bold gestures in their presentations.
- *Level contact.*
  Where do we pitch our material, at what level, in terms of an audience of engineers?

Having examined various aspects to do with *contact*, let us look at other aspects which may crucially affect our presentation.

Leaking our feelings through non-verbal behaviours

These are feelings that we tend to give off when we are communicating. What 'leaks' do you give off when you make a presentation? Do you appear bored or worried and does that show? Do you appear acutely nervous and does that show? Do you send out 'help' me signals by the way you glance at your watch and shuffle your notes about?

Here is another very good reason for you to look up and around at your audience: you will be in a better position to 'read' their leakage and if it is not very favourable do something about it such as cutting things short, going over a point again in a different way, stopping to add an example, etc. This also explains why it would be unwise to read the whole speech word for word. Remember though that the occasional negative leakage such as a member of your audience yawning may in fact be that you haven't opened the window and it's getting very stuffy.

Congruence or matching. What you say and how you say it

This is the matching or lack of it between the verbal and the non-verbal signals that you send out while you are giving the presentation.

An example of this would be if our speaker in his or her talk about client care in the engineering industry had felt very enthusiastic about something and had used words such a *'new, vital, crucial, essential'* but the tone of voice these words are delivered is very flat – no emphasis or tonal variety. The audience will probably then think that he did not believe this to be very new or crucial or essential.

In other words the non-verbal and the verbal must match, there must be some kind of congruence otherwise our doubts are roused and we tend to think the speaker lacks conviction. Now it is possible to go over the top here and so rant and roar with conviction that the audience will think you are (a) not serious and taking the mickey, (b) too serious and totally full of missionary zeal – this can be a real turn-off. In general, many American presenters may appear to British audiences as being rather 'over the top'. Their enthusiasm may incur diminishing returns in terms of sustaining an audience's attention.

Humour contact

Appropriacy is the key word here. It is essential to match the humour with the kind of audience that will be listening to it. Most people think of jokes when they think of humour in presentations. There are obvious risks associated with the use of jokes. One, the audience may well have heard it before. The presenter is then greeted with that awful sigh or groan which is a real killer to your confidence. Secondly, the audience may fail to see the humour or see how it relates to what you are going to say. Unless you are experienced and confident in telling jokes, our advice would be to make use of anecdotes, personal to you, or those that have happened to others, to illustrate the points you wish to make. It is vital at the start of the presentation to adjust your humour to the mood of your audience. You need to have them on your side; an inapproprioate joke, story or attempt at humour will mean that you may lose some completely and put off others for a long time. The first minutes of your talk will then become a desperate effort to win that audience back to your side.

❑ Start to keep a scrapbook of cuttings from the newspapers, cartoons, sayings, stories, etc., that you can make use of in future presentations.

Although it doesn't strictly come under 'contact' we should mention at this point how to respond to questions.

Handling questions

Getting questions is one sign that you have been listened to. The important thing is to know how to handle them. Basically you have the following choices:

- Ignore the question. Inadvisable; it appears rude and your questioner may well come back even more forcefully.
- Delay the question. Do that if you are not ready to take it, i.e. it comes in the middle of what you're saying. (Remember if you say at the start of your presentation: 'by the way if there's anything you want to ask me just do that,' then you are running a risk of being interrupted in mid-flow.) Just say to your questioner: 'Excuse me I'd like to answer that later when I've reached that point.'
- Answer the question. If you can, straight away but if you can't, do say that and promise to come back to the questioner when you've found out. It is fatal to try and waffle your way through an answer.

You can make use of a question to add further information to your presentation, provided you remain conscious of time and how it is passing. Avoid if possible taking a second question from the same person unless you are certain that no one else wants to join in.

Checklist of presentation skills

To finish, here is a checklist that you might find useful when carrying self-assessment on your own presentations or when assisting a colleague.

	(5 high, 1 low)				
Content					
Shows knowledge of subject and presents it at appropriate level	1	2	3	4	5
Contact					
Eye contact with audience	1	2	3	4	5
Audibility	1	2	3	4	5
Variety of vocal delivery	1	2	3	4	5
Degree of enthusiasm	1	2	3	4	5
Quality of introduction	1	2	3	4	5
Quality of conclusion	1	2	3	4	5
Structure of talk	1	2	3	4	5
Use of visual aids	1	2	3	4	5
Time keeping (agreed limits)	1	2	3	4	5

You might like to adapt this checklist for your own use. In your presentations there may be particular criteria that you would wish to emphasize.

That ends this section of making a presentation. In the next chapter we look at the skills required in presenting to smaller groups – at seminars and meetings.

Summary

- When preparing for any presentation always try and take into consideration your audience's likely attitudes and expectations to you and your subject. Try and angle your material to these.
- It's very important for you to project a positive image. Remember the audience will 'want' you to succeed because failure is so embarrassing.
- Brainstorming around the topic to be presented can reveal unexpected angles and prevent you from becoming boring and boring yourself. This is especially the case if you have to give the talk several times.
- With an audience that is negative in its outlook, keep the presentation brief, provide good examples to back up your case.
- Never apologize for your lack of skill, time or experience.
- Prepare speech notes with just key points on them, not an essay!
- Put in some rough timings as you rehearse your talk. These should help you in keeping to your allotted limits.
- Remember a presentation is about building a relationship with your audience, so do look at them.
- Try and get verbal and non-verbal matching. If your message is positive, then make it sound and appear so.
- Think about contact with the audience both in the presentation and the questions that follow it. Don't ignore a question. Do your best to answer it. If you don't know the answer, don't flannel, say you'll find out.

Useful further reading

R Ellis and A McClintock (1994) *If You Take My Meaning*. Arnold.
C T Goodworth (1984) *Effective Presentation*. Business Books.
C Turk (1985) *Effective Speaking*. E & F N Spon.

9

Committees and meetings

We point out the responsibilities of the individual as a participant in groups; we identify some of the common problems with many meetings and provide techniques and approaches to assist the chairperson. We identify the key criteria that may transform a group into a team and suggest a method which may help reduce the stresses and strains inside any group.

Introduction

You will be involved in meetings – hundreds and hundreds of them – all through your life as an engineer. If you are a student reading this then no doubt you've already had a fair number under your belt, especially if you've been involved in your students' union or departmental staff–student liaison committees.

Before we get down to detail there is one very important aspect to always bear in mind. As soon as someone says 'meeting', and he or she starts reaching for the diary to pin you down to a date, please stop for one minute and think: do we actually need a meeting for this?

So many people have a kind of automatic reaction to the word meeting. They reach for their diaries and start scribbling in the time and place without ever stopping to consider if there is a need for one? After all there's fax, the telephone, informal chats in the corridor or over coffee. Increasingly, there are other alternatives including teleconferencing. However, if the answer, after some pause for thought is, 'Yes, we do need to meet', then we have to consider how to get the very best out of the time we will be setting aside. For tips as to how to do this, please read on.

You as a participant

The most important first question to ask when someone invites you to go on a committee is: 'What is my role and what is expected of me?' This is rather a similar question to the one we recommend you ask when it came to making a presentation (page 67) – what is the topic and what will my audience expect of me?

Unless you have this question answered then it is very difficult for you ever to be confident when attending a meeting. You will sit there and when it comes to participation – asking questions and making a contribution – you will find it much more difficult to act confidently.

> ❏ So do clarify your role at the meeting, within the group. Ask yourself: 'Am I attending this meeting as one or more of the following?'

Representative

You represent a group, i.e. convenor of the hang-gliding club on the SCR (Student Representative Council). Your role is to represent your members' wishes – they want a take-off point from the top of the engineering lab.

Delegate

You have been delegated to act on others' behalf, i.e. to vote for them. This same club has decided at its meeting that you should vote against the proposal to ban all student parties from the top of the engineering lab on warm summer evenings!

Observer

You are at the meeting purely to observe the participants. This is a new committee and you are an experienced hand and they want some helpful advice on committee procedures – that's going to be your job.

Expert

Called to attend by reason of your expertise in a particular field (i.e. a structural engineer might well be called in to give evidence at a planning meeting). You as an expert hang-'glidist' have been asked to speak to the Sports Council planning committee on your sport being given recognition at the next Olympic Games!

Consultant

Similar to the expert but one who attends over a series of meetings. For example, the proposal that hang-gliding become an Olympic sport having been ratified, there will be a need to plan a strategy – this is where you come in. Your job is to mastermind the strategy; you bring in the expertise.

Secretary

Non-participating: your job is to take minutes of the meeting and not to participate.

Minutes taker

Participating: there not only to take minutes but also join in any discussion (as far as you can). This is always difficult; the best way to do it is to talk your dilemma through with the chairperson. If there are particular issues that you want to speak to then perhaps someone else could take over the job for that particular period. The more you can work with your chair the easier your job will be. See pages 134–137 for further information on minute taking.

Chair

More of your role later in this chapter.

Having clarified your role you then need to do some preparation before the meeting. This could include:

- Reading through previous minutes to see what are the current issues.
- Checking in the minutes and with the organizer (or chairman) that you are not required to perform anything 'special' at the meeting – such as a presentation, provision of facts etc. It can be very embarrassing when you turn over the page to see against your club's name *Presentation to Committee* written there in the action column.
- Checking through the agenda so that if you are a representative you will be prepared. There may be an issue coming up at the next meeting on which your members would have a direct interest. It would be helpful to take some soundings in case it came to a vote.

What goes wrong with so many meetings?

You've probably got your own storehouse of treasured memories: those blissful moments when you've so enjoyed listening to that so fascinating discussion on how to redesign the lower flange of the upper crocket, sipping that so delicious cold coffee in that beautifully air reconditioned room, so carried away that you never thought about the papers stacking up and all those things to see to!

Here's a few of ours:

- They overrun. This is a new form of relativity: clocks in meetings run slower!
- They get into a muddle – too many people are speaking at the same time.
- The agenda is not followed: '*I thought we'd been over this before?*'
- No actions, outcomes or conclusions are determined.
- No one appears to be taking any notes/minutes of actions agreed.
- There is confusion as to who is supposed to be doing what, when and for whom?
- The room gets very stuffy/cold/noisy.
- The chair keeps missing out key people who should speak but who aren't very confident.

And that's just for starters!

So what can we as participants do about these faults. Are we to sit there powerless, getting increasingly frustrated?

We've said we need to do that essential pre-meeting series of checks about our roles and therefore others' expectations.

You can make suggestions

Simple ones such as 'Could we have a window open?', 'Would this be a time for a short break?', 'Would it be possible to move this table a little to the left as it's difficult to see the speaker'. These are simple interventions but they may well make a tremendous difference to the successful outcome of the meeting. If you do pluck up courage to make this kind of suggestion you will very often find that others sitting round you hoped that someone would pipe up.

You can help the chair

Ask tactfully at which point on the agenda the meeting's at. Suggest a change in order to accommodate those who have to leave early and need to speak; suggest moving the less important items to the end, having a short break if things get heated, reminding the group about the constitution (We cannot have more than five members on committee at any one time, but we could co-opt someone.)

Stay alert and be observant

If you do you will be able to spot when the meeting drifts way from the topic under discussion. Use a phrase such as: *'Chairman, I think someone over here had a point'* (you can see someone struggling to be noticed). *'Chairman aren't we missing the deadline for this decision?'* As an observant participant you can also note when you feel the balance of the meeting has been upset – one person or one section or one interest or view seems to be getting more than a fair ration of the available time.

Speak up and make your point clearly and concisely

Avoid waffling and repeating yourself. Keep what you have to say to the point being discussed on the agenda.

Use humour and tact to keep the temperature from overheating

Humour can defuse so many awkward situations.

> *'Chairman: I think our spirits are beginning to sag over this matter. I suggest that we adjourn to the bar.'*

You may think this is all rather outlandish especially if you are a student but let's face it – how many times do we blame the organizers or the chairman for the rotten experience we are having at another boring meeting when to some extent the remedy lies in our own hands as a participant? It is really about being assertive and remembering the points we made in Chapter 3.

Yourself as chair

You may already have had experience of being in the chair. For many it is rather a fearsome time. It is such a difficult job that it is very unfair ever to plunge someone straight in at the deep end without providing them with any support, coaching or training. If you know you are likely to become chairman/chairperson/madam chair (you may have been given official recognition of this impending step by being made vice-chairman), do ask to chair a portion of the meeting while the regular chair or experienced members of the committee are there to provide you with advice and support. If you know you are going to be vice-chair or chair then do take very careful note next time you are at a meeting to see how they get on, the kinds of skills they employ or fail to.

Activity

Think back to the times you've been at meetings and the various chairpersons you've observed. What are the key ingredients that you think make for good chairing?

Here are some of ours:

- *Never come into the meeting late.*
  It gives a very poor impression and it means that you will not be in a position to be proactive; proactive in this case means that you plan the agenda. This could involve you in:
- *Prepare thoroughly beforehand.*
  Think through the various items of business, their priorities and roughly how much time to allot to each. These allotments can and should be negotiated with the committee but it is desirable that you as chair have some notions in your own mind.

  Other kinds of pre-meeting preparation could include: seeing to the room, chairs, tables, paper work, etc.
- *Preserve some kind of balance at the meeting.*
  Think of the proceedings as in fact a chair. Your aim as chair is to preserve some kind of balance between the various 'legs' these represent the various persons and their various interests gathered round the table – you don't want the discussion to become unbalanced. If this happens then you will find that those who feel that they haven't been given a reasonable

chance to have their say may well 'sulk' and take no further part or become hostile and argumentative. Neither of these actions is conducive to healthy meetings.

Keep a mental or physical note of where the contributions are coming from. This is one area where you as a participant can influence the meeting in a most positive way.

- *Progress the meeting*
They often get bogged down and fail to go anywhere. This is one very good reason for the chairperson to do his or her homework before the meeting begins. It is also vital to plan some kind of structure to each item under discussion. Keep a sense of progress. Don't get bogged down in detail. If you are planning a conference don't let someone start rabbiting on about whether there should be brown or white toast served for breakfast to the delegates! If you think this is far fetched then you haven't been to many meetings as yet!

- *Consider the environment.*
Assess the layout of tables and chairs, provision of papers, lighting, heating, ventilation, provision of water, coffee, etc. Someone else may do this for you but you will need to see that these environmental factors are planned for.

S.AP.S.A. – think SAPSA

- **S** stands for **setting**. Set the topic or have someone else do it.
For example:

'Let's now move to item 3. Last meeting we examined how ... this is the time now to make a decision.'

Or

'The item's concerning conference 199 ... I've asked Susan to give us an overview of where we are with the planning. After Susan has finished we will open it for general discussion. We must however have some decision by the end of today.'

This setting of the scene is very valuable; many chairpersons do not do it or if they do they mumble it through. All those round the table should fully understand what the item is and what they are supposed to be discussing together with some guide as to how they are to discuss it. They should also be aware of any constraints such as deadlines; if this happens then there should be less floundering and time wasting.

- **AP** stands for **active participation**. Why have a meeting unless everyone is prepared to participate in some way. Participation can refer to providing information, asking questions, reminding everyone about procedure – in fact all the aspects we listed earlier.

- **S** stands for **summary**. After the active participation we need a time for a summary to pull things together. This is a part of the chairperson's job that is so often missing. A summary of the main points discussed can help those present to focus in on the key points. This is especially valuable if there is to be any voting involved. People should be very clear as to exactly what it is they are voting for.
- **A** stands for **action**. Here we have the conclusions reached, the actions to be taken. All too often people leave a meeting uncertain as to what has been achieved. You hear at the end ominous mutterings *'Are you supposed to?' 'Who is to carry out the ...?', 'What did we decide to do about ...?'*.

Such confusion should be avoided if time is spent at the end of each item of business pulling out the bullet points. It is extremely useful at the conclusion of the whole meeting for a summary to be given. If you have to take minutes of the meeting you will find these helpful to you in shaping your notes.

Being a chair of a committee is then a very onerous job. It requires support, encouragement, coaching and training. Don't be tempted to plunge right in.

Teams and groups

The first question to ask is: do the individual members of the group feel a team or are they a number of individuals? Are they, in a football analogy, all strikers with no one back in defence?

TEAM is often translated in management development books as **T**ogether **E**ach **A**chieves **M**ore. You are/have been a member of a team whether it be sporting, social, work or within the forces, boy scouting or guides. As a student you will no doubt be part of some team. Would you for instance call the present department of engineering that you are in a team, or your current third year, or perhaps the section of that year? Do these groups feel like teams? Do they behave as though they are part of a team?

Activity

What are your criteria for a team? What, in your opinion, distinguishes a team from merely a collection of individuals?

Would you include some or all of these?

- Some consensus as to the aims and the goals of the team.
- Good reliable and open communication between members of that team.
- Some clarity of individual roles and responsibilities within the team.
- Some attempt at review of the team so that it doesn't become stale.
- Leadership which suits where the team is at in terms of its maturity. Sometimes this leadership will be very direct (i.e. there's no point quibbling

about lack of participation if there's a bomb threat. Someone tells you to jump and you jump. On the other hand, after the immediate crisis has passed, the leadership could be much more participative by having a review of emergency procedures and by tapping individual ideas.

- A sense of challenge – individual members don't feel they are rusting away.
- Some fun and excitement; it shouldn't be all deadly serious and ever so earnest.

We are sure that you could add a number of other features from your own experience of being in a 'good team'. You might have included such things as the wearing of team uniform, having a shared locality, speaking the same kind of in-language.

Communication to keep a team healthy

A healthy team is one where individuals feel good about themselves and about their team. Where there is poor communication – either too little or too much of the wrong kind – then the team can begin to go downhill and morale suffers. *'We weren't told anything. Why is it that you lot seem to hear everything that's going and no one ever bothers to tell us?'*

We recommend this little exercise for all teams. It is similar to an engine overhaul. If it is done on a regular basis then there won't be seizure and the progress of the team coming to a grinding halt. It takes us back to Tuchman's concept of storming which we examined on page 58.

Get the members of the team round a table and put down on a blackboard or flip chart the questions:

```
What are some of the factors that are helping us work as a
team?

  •  ------------------------------------------------------------
  •  ------------------------------------------------------------
  •  ------------------------------------------------------------

What are some of the factors, if any, which may be
reducing our effectiveness as a team?

  •  ------------------------------------------------------------
  •  ------------------------------------------------------------
  •  ------------------------------------------------------------

What can we do about these?
```

We are not suggesting that this process will solve all your team problems but going through such an exercise should help to expose troubles before they fester to become something worse. You know how it is with teams, little things can annoy, little complaints can grow into something bigger. By going through this kind of review process then these can be exposed to some fresh air and hopefully cured.

A word of caution: if you as a team decide to go through this kind of exercise don't just do it and then forget all about the outcomes. If you do it will breed cynicism about such procedures.

> *'Well we all went through this rigmarole and what happened – nothing, not one decision after all those promises!'*

Secondly, if the temperature in the group is chilly and there is a likelihood of very real criticism to the team leader then it is often a good idea to bring in a neutral chairman or facilitator to conduct the session. Having such a person can take the personal sting out of the criticism and lead it into more constructive channels.

Other ways of developing communication within the team

There are all kinds of techniques to develop communication – everything from newsletters to electronic sign boards. However, the simple truth is that no matter how excellent are the systems of communication they will not be attended to by those who are supposed to take note unless the listeners, readers and watchers have faith and trust in the communication. So much time and money has been wasted in organizations who have gone in for beautifully printed staff newsletters and how sad to see them thrown away or just left about without any signs that they have been opened and actually read.

Activity

What are some of the key factors that we should keep in mind when designing a communication system for our teams? Draw up a list before you read ours.

- Is it trustworthy? Will members of the group take note of the information because they believe in it?
- Is it timely? Does the information arrive when members of the team need it? There's little point sending out your newsletter days or weeks after the events have occurred. Your credibility as a source of information will rapidly diminish if members of your team hear about some change to their organization from someone on a bus or as a news item in their local paper!
- Is it understandable? Can the members of the team actually understand what is printed, put on the notice board, etc. (We will examine this element in our section 'Put it in writing', pages 97–100.)

This is particularly the case with short forms, abbreviations, etc. Furthermore, all notices must be free from ambiguity, e.g. not this kind of writing:

```
All members of the team are reminded that our labs will be
inspected on Thursday. Please make sure that procedures are
fully in place.
```

You can imagine the state of confusion this could throw the team into. Does Thursday refer to this coming one? Which procedures are being referred to?

- Is the communication efficient? Does it warrant the effort involved in organizing the communication, the person or persons who have to word process the draft, the efforts and costs involved in printing and distribution? Taking all this into account will it be worthwhile? Will it be effective as communication?

Short-term groups. Task teams

Increasingly in engineering, people may well find themselves members of short-term groups. These will be formed for a specific purpose, with a specific remit and deadline and then will die. Engineers will increasingly find themselves occupying different roles in different teams. In one he or she might act as team leader, in another as specialist, in another as co-ordinator for various subgroups. Tom Peters, the management guru, has remarked that organizations will increasingly resemble amoebas in their structure; rigid lines of demarcation between individuals in terms of hierarchies, departments, sections will lessen. Individuals will occupy different niches according to the demand for their skills. This is where we come back to the Belbin model: the technical role (expert) and the team role (personal qualities).

Bill Gates of Microsoft believes very much in these loose amoeba-like structures. These are more flexible, less rigid, more easy to change in a time of rapid change. His company is built on such loose flat structures.

One theory is that Amundsen reached the Pole before Captain Scott because his team was 'loose' whereas the British team was rigid. In the Norwegian tent there was plenty of discussion as to plans for the Pole, arguments and 'storming'. Amundsen at one point was the leader pushing ahead, at another he moved to the side to allow one of the experts (on dog handling or navigation) to lead. Captain Scott's tent was less noisy. There was little discussion as to who would go to the Pole; the decision to take five men on the final journey came as a surprise. There was only one leader and that was Scott.

Naturally we cannot take such an analogy too far. Many engineering companies have had to 're-engineer' themselves so as to allow for more flexibility, more sensitivity in reacting to the needs of their customers. This has meant redesigning the structures of organizations, reviewing individual roles and removing some of the barriers between sections, creating looser, flatter workplaces.

Summary

- Crucial for your success as a participant at a meeting is clarification of your role.
- Participants at a meeting, and not just the chair, have a direct responsibility for the success of that meeting. They can check on the agenda, assist others to participate, keep discussion relevant, provide helpful advice, etc.
- Chairpersons need to prepare carefully before the meeting – the items on the agenda, the ordering of discussions, etc.
- SAPSA is a structure that might help: S, setting; AP, active participation; S, summarize key points leading to A, Action.
- For groups to become teams they must share a clear aim and understanding of roles and responsibilities.
- Review of teams' progress can assist team morale; if caught early enough such reviews can prevent minor irritations becoming large scale eruptions.
- There are various aspects to be borne in mind when developing a communication system for a group: it must be reliable, timely, and clearly understood.
- Increasingly rigid hierarchical structures are being replaced by looser, flatter team structures. At any one time an individual may play different roles in different teams.

Further reading

T Peters and N Austin (1994) *A Passion for Excellence*. Harper Collins.
R Semler (1993) *Maverick*. Arrow.

Part IV

Part IV

10

Introduction to writing skills

In this chapter we examine some of the criteria we could use when assessing writing and at those features which make writing different from oral communication.

Introduction

Is there something special about writing? Is there something about this skill that makes it different when compared to speaking?

For one thing it is often thought by the reader to be *deliberate and intentional* – done with a purpose. So much speech is rapid, spontaneous and 'throw away' unless it happens to be within a formal setting such as an interview, meeting, public speech, or business telephone call.

When we sit down to read a fax, word processed report, letter, then provided it is put into formal English we will normally consider that it has been deliberately done; that the writer meant what he or she said. We don't really know whether this was the case or whether the text was knocked out with scarcely a moment's thought, but most readers will probably consider this not to have been the case – especially where it has been printed and not hand-written. The very fact of print, and now almost invariably laser print, implies deliberation of purpose and intention behind the act of composition compared to a scrappy note left lying around.

When we write formal letters, reports, etc. our readers will normally think that what we have done has been *deliberate*. This means that we have to take great care of the words we use, the accuracy of what we write and also the tone and manner of how we write it. Once it's sitting on their desk we can't very well disown it. We can't very well phone up and say, *'Well I didn't actually mean what I said in the letter – it just came out – very sorry'*.

Activity

We've already mentioned a few criteria for effective writing; can you add to the list?

Let's start with those aspects of the text that first might 'hit' you as you start reading. You pick up the text and are immediately aware of:

- Has it got my name on it or that of my department or organization?
- Language – English or some other.
- Black/white or colour.
- Size of print and appearance of print on page.
- Illustrations, tables, drawings, maps.
- Paragraphs, numbers in margin, on top, bottom of page, headings.
- Type of English – formal, informal, modern, old fashioned – serious, humorous.
- Tone – does it annoy me, please me?
- Dates when written, author/s, origins.
- Spelling.
- Grammar.
- Punctuation.
- Length of sentences.
- Clarity of sentences – abbreviations.
- Flow and links between sentences.
- Argument, reasoning, evidence.
- Comparisons with other texts.
- Sense of general readability/interest – 'getting somewhere'.
- Use of illustrations – tables clearly laid out or muddled, pie charts that are clear and communicate something useful?

We're not suggesting that this is the only route that a reader may cover when first meeting a text; much will depend on his or her motivation, experience with similar texts, time available (i.e. a leisurely perusal or a snatched rapid look), quality of light, comfort of reader, external noises, level, degree of knowledge of specialized forms and language, etc. We all have our own 'thing' when it comes to writing, rather in the same way that we all have our own 'thing' when it comes to speech – *'I just don't like that accent'*.

The same kind of prejudices surround the written word. Some people have very fixed views on handwriting. They look critically to see if the writing slopes too far right, if the Ts are crossed firmly and if there is a consistency about the height of the letters. Then there are a host of other prejudices concerning the kind of pen used – ballpoints are considered to be second rate to ink pens by some; oblique nibs to others may show an artistic streak, etc. We look at these aspects on pages 110–111 in dealing with letters of application. As a general rule we can say that in order to impress people reading your hand-written script you'd always be better advised to write with a bold hand using an ink or felt-tip pen with blue/black or black ink, rather than thin ballpoint, pencil or very thick faint felt tip in purple, green or mauve.

So back to our scanning of a written document. Pick up a report, a text of any kind. Which route do you go along as you start to read. Do your eyes scan the overall picture before you focus into the detail? What attracts or repels you as far as the text and its arrangement on the page is concerned? (We will be looking at some aspects of reading and how you can become a more efficient reader on pages 133–135.)

Writing is more permanent than speech

The second aspect of writing that we should consider is the fact that it lasts longer than speech – it doesn't perish as fast, that is unless the words spoken are particularly powerful, catch us on the raw or evoke some deep and powerful memory.

The fact that writing is more permanent – it becomes a record – again means that we have to take much more care when we are drafting our reports and letters. Minutes of a meeting can be cited in a court of law. Damages have been awarded because of what someone has written about someone else in a letter or newspaper column. Civil damages have been brought against the writer of a report whose conclusions and recommendation proved disastrous.

In speech we can usually apologize when we have hit the wrong tone and we can normally correct something which the listener has picked up in a way that was never intended.

With writing however we are caught. Its very apparent deliberate nature and its permanence (in relative terms) means that we can't get away with much. We have to be careful. We have to check carefully what we write. We have to edit the text with great care before it reaches our readers.

We have already quoted from Earnest Gowers' book *Plain Words*. It is still in print and has had an enormous influence in the development of plain English. We list it in the further reading at the end of this section. In it Gowers quoted a sentence which we feel sums up our argument:

'Put yourself in your reader's shoes.'

This is advice we strongly recommend. Before you start to write and especially before you send off that final draft, ask yourself this question: what will my reader think of this?

Writing in its context

This leads us to the third distinctive aspect of writing: that we have to remember that our reader will read it in its context. He or she may have already met us, or members of our company, have developed some opinion of us (positive or negative) and so will read not only the lines but between them. For example, it's no good writing that the company is

'very distressed to hear that ...'

when all previous contacts with the customer have shown very little interest or commitment to serving that particular customer's needs. Reading between the lines it doesn't sound as if they're very distressed, more likely couldn't be that bothered. So always try and put yourself in the reader's shoes. Ask whether he or she will find these words convincing given the context, the setting and relationships. We will see further example of this on page 141.

On several occasions in this book we have mentioned the importance of cultural aspects in communication. In writing we should remember that when we are sending a letter to another country we should adopt styles and conventions which will not offend. We discuss this in more detail in our next chapter on letter writing when we look at the difficulties that might be present when a British engineer writes to his or her counterpart in France.

Summary

- Writing appears to be considered a more deliberate communication act than speech. For that reason it may be more influential both positively and negatively. Great care therefore needs to be taken with such matters as accuracy of facts, proof-reading to eliminate errors and the tone in which it is put.
- We need to put ourselves in our reader's shoes so that we can gauge the effect of our writing. This may be particularly relevant when it comes to cross-cultural written communication.

Further reading

R Ellis and K Hopkins (1985) *How to Succeed in Written Work and Study*. Collins.
E Gowers (1987) *Plain Words*. Penguin.
C Turk and J Kirkman (1982) *Effective Writing*. E & F N Spon.
R Barrass (1987) *Scientists Must Write*. Chapman & Hall.

11

The letter

In this chapter we provide advice on the layout and structuring of letters. Particular attention is paid to making sure that your letters has the appropriate tone and style for your reader. Various examples of letters of complaint and application are provided.

Introduction

You will be familiar with letters, so many pour through our letter boxes every day. However, because of their importance it's worthwhile taking the time to write them properly. It might be that in these days of electronic mail and the Internet that the paper-based letter is of even greater importance. This takes us back to our discussion of redundancy and entropy which we encountered on page 7.

The word 'influence' should be on your mind as you think of letters – and we are referring to business letters A to B, from engineer to client. Naturally letters carry information but they do a great deal more: they also carry influence. A letter is part of your personal relations – your PR and marketing. Consider when you have read a letter from some organization and it has been poorly produced, perhaps misspelled and difficult to fathom what the writer was getting at; what did it do for your estimation of that organization?

Here's the opening of a letter that was given to the author – the name of the organization has been changed for obvious reasons but the material in the text is genuine. It is a letter from a computer company to a customer who complained of delay in the delivery of a PC.

> **Activity**
>
> What do you think of it as a specimen? Read it through carefully.

```
Dear Sir,

I write with reference to your correspondence dated 6th
February 1996 regarding your PC, as always I was very
concerned to receive this type of letter from any
customer.

I must firstly apologise for the delay in getting your
computer to you, it was an extremely busy period before
and just after the New Year break. Certainly the sales
team were working through the night so that we could
honour our scheldues, however a small percentage of our
customers did experience a delay such as yours for which
the company is very sorry about.

I enclose vouchers which will entitle you to discounts on
your next purchase with us.

Yours sincerely
```

Did you spot all the errors and deficiencies?

You can see the effect this would have on any reader. The aim of this letter remember is to apologize for a lapse in service; you would think that the writer would be on his or her very best writing behaviour. A positive, well-written letter in response to a complaint cannot only put matters right as far as the immediate complaint is concerned (the informational side) but also start the 'healing' process so that the reader gains an enhanced impression of the said organization.

Remember too that any letter written for the attention of one person may well get passed on to others, so that it is a kind of ambassador for you and for your organization.

Activity

Here is a possible re-write of that letter. If you were the Sales Manager of the said company would you sign it or would you want to make further changes?

```
Dear Mr X,

                Late delivery of personal computer

Thank you for your letter of 6th February 1996. We are
sorry that you experienced such poor service from us and
would like to offer you our apologies.

Although the New Year break is a very busy period you
should have received your computer by the 15th of January.
We have since found out that your order was incorrectly
filed with others; this explains the delay. We are very
sorry this has happened. We have, as a result of this
error, completely re-organized our system for recording
orders.

To help compensate for this inconvenience you were caused
please accept the enclosed vouchers, these will entitle you
to discounts on your next purchase from us. We look
forward to meeting your computer needs in the future.

Please phone me on this direct number (01234-6578) if
there is anything I can help you with over this matter.
```

Did you think this revised letter provides:

- the information: i.e. why the product did not reach the customer
- the PR: we are a good organization to deal with even though we do occasionally make mistakes; at least we learn from them and have the interest of our customers firmly at heart!

Structuring your letter

The reason for supplying a clear structure in a letter is very much the same as we will state when we come to reports; our readers want to get the gist of what we are about; they want to be able to glance along the sheet of paper and be able to abstract the key ideas without having to plough their way through a thicket of dense prose. One way we can help is by putting in bold the topic we are writing about at the top of the letter. This normally comes after the 'salutation' – the Dear Sir.

Think **TRAP (Topic, Reaction, Action, Polite Close)**

T for TOPIC – our first paragraph after the title should establish exactly why we want our reader to read our letter. In many business letters it is often one main topic divided up into several sub-topics.

It is important to read very carefully any previous correspondence to establish what exactly are the various topics that are needing to be addressed. You know how infuriating it is when you have taken the time and trouble to compose a letter setting out your views, your complaints, etc., only to read the answering letter and find that few if any of these points have in fact been answered. This is one of the problems of standard letters, precisely because they are standard they cannot be flexible enough to provide a satisfactory answer to letters of request, complaint and enquiry. They cannot easily differentiate between different kinds of customers.

Activity

Here is an example of setting out a topic in a letter. Do you think it clearly sets this out? What changes would you make if you were the Student Rep?

```
The Contracts Manager
Cut Up Rough Engineering
Leeds                                    Nov 5th 1996

Dear Contracts Manager

You were kind enough to come to the Civil Engineering
Department of Faraday University to speak to students
taking the special option on Law and The Engineer.
You did say that it would be possible to organize a follow
up visit to your firm to talk through with you and members
of your team some of the particular issues that you didn't
have time to cover in your talk. As Student Rep I have
been asked if it would be possible to arrange such a
visit. We would be particularly interested in looking at
some details of contracts with local government that you
said were particularly awkward at this time of re-
organization.
```

Did the writer set out the topic clearly and concisely so that the reader can gain at a glance what he or she has to do?

Compare this possible re-write:

Dear Contracts Manager

Visit by Students of Faraday University

I am writing as Student Rep of the Civil Engineering Department at the above institution to ask you whether we could take you up on the kind offer you made after your lecture on April 25th.

You suggested that our class might visit your company at some mutually convenient time. The purpose would be to discuss with you and your colleagues some of the issues that you face in terms of handling contracts from local government. This you suggested was becoming a real problem for civil engineers due mainly to recent local government reorganization and subsequent confusion over awarding and vetting contracts.

Do you feel this better sets out the topic – the intention of the letter?

R stands for your response. Having made sure that you send a clear signal to the reader that you have understood the position then you will need to spell out exactly what kind of actions you and your organization propose to take. Increasingly in this section you may have to spell out.

A stands for action. Sometimes these two paragraphs or parts of the letter would be joined together, i.e. the response is the action. However, there may be a separate response section: this is the stage where you set out the action or conclusion so that your reader can be in no doubt what is to happen. Such phrases as: 'we intend'; 'therefore we can now'; 'we are prepared therefore to offer you', etc.

P stands for the polite close. No matter how upset and annoyed you are with your correspondent this must not show. Keep cool!

We are not saying that this structure can be applied to all situations, for instance it might be possible to move from topic to action without any consideration of response. Over the page is a complete letter written to this structure and in reply to the letter we quoted earlier. What do you think of it?

> Dear Dave
>
> Thank you for your letter of February 13th. I should be very pleased to welcome you and your fellow students to our company. The date of Wednesday May 15th at 2pm would be suitable.
>
> As I said in my lecture we do a great deal of work with local government. The recent change to the structure of local government has made the winning of contracts for civil engineering work very much more difficult. I suggest that it would be useful if you as representative for the others could collect some questions arising from my talk which you would like me and my colleagues to try and answer during the session. If you could fax these to us a day or so before the visit then we would have time to put our heads together and think up some answers – If we can! I will arrange for the board room to be made available from 2–4 pm. Coffee and tea will be served at 3 pm. There is a Partners' meeting at 4 pm, so my colleagues and I would have to finish the session by 4 pm. I'm sure that will give us enough time to chew the fat.
>
> I have asked Roger Brown our contracts manager to attend; he has had a great deal of experience in this area.
>
> I look forward to receiving the questions – don't make them too hard – and meeting you at our offices.
>
> Yours sincerely

Questions to ask:

- Is it well structured for easy reading?
- Does it fully answer the letter from the students' rep?
- Does it provide sufficient detail for him to prepare his party?
- Is it business like but friendly as appropriate from a senior engineer to a student. Is the humour appropriate?

Having looked at the structure we should now review the actual layout.

Layout of letters

The layout of your letter is designed to make the reading task easier for your reader. Basically there are two standard layouts, with several variations. Which one you will adopt will depend on the 'house style' of the organization you represent or if self-employed the one you have decided to use.

Traditional

Use this style for any hand-written letters. Note the indented paragraphs.

```
                                              Your address
Their name and designation
Their address

Reference                                     Date

Salutation (Dear)

                     Possible heading
     _____

_____
_____
_____
_____

     _____
_____
_____
_____

     Subscription (Yours, etc.)

                   Signature
```

Blocked

```
Your Name/designation
Organization
Address
Telephone/fax

Ref. and date

Reader's name and
address


Salutation
```

Possible heading

_____
_____
_____
_____

_____
_____
_____
_____

_____
_____

_____
_____
_____
_____

Subscription (Yours, etc.)

Signature

Style in letters

Layout and structure is reasonably simple compared with the complexities of style. The most important thing to remember is that the style should be appropriate to the situation, the context in which you are writing. For example Hi Bill, Dear Sir, Dear Dr Smithson.

'*Having a great time*', is a most appropriate style for a postcard but not for a business letter. '*Dear Sir*' would not be very appropriate if you were corresponding with someone in an organization you had developed some kind of relationship with.

Examine this opening to a letter. The context is that the recipient has recently been interviewed for a job and has failed to get it.

```
Dear Sir,

It is regretted that the Board were unable to recommend
that your name go forward for appointment.

We thank you for your application.
```

We said in the introduction to writing that *tone* was very important when it came to all aspects of written text. In letters your reader will be reading between the lines and therefore it is very important to read the text as if in the position of your reader. Try and place yourself where he or she would be as they open that envelope.

As we mentioned earlier (page 99) there's no point in writing '*We were very distressed to hear about the problem that you had with your electricity supply*', if it is obvious to both parties and especially the reader that the quality of the service provided left so much in terms of quality of performance that they couldn't be *distressed*. This ability to put yourself inside our reader's shoes is a very important dimension to being a successful writer of letters.

Activity

Over the page is a possible re-write of that letter of refusal. Do you think it now does the job?

> Dear Mr Thomas
>
> Thank you for attending the interview for the post of … on July 24th. We were impressed with your application but do not feel able to recommend your appointment to the Board. We realize that you will be disappointed. The choice was very difficult for the panel.
>
> Thank you for your interest in the organization. If you would like to phone on extension 215 we could supply you with feedback on your application.

Letters of application

This is a very special kind of letter and one which deserves special treatment. It is very much a marketing exercise in which *you* are the product. This letter and possibly the enclosed CV (see page 116) will, you hope, unlock the gates surrounding the interview and allow you through.

Remember that all such letters will be read quickly to scan out the essential information (your qualifications, etc.). Increasingly with large companies that regularly receive hundreds if not thousands of applications, especially for those junior management posts geared to graduates, computers are doing this task. It makes very good sense therefore to make sure that this essential information is clearly set out.

Applications letters should in general be:

- short and very much to the point – a single page
- well set out – clearly paragraphed
- very carefully proof-read to ensure that all errors – spelling, punctuation are spotted and put right.

Do make certain that your contact address and phone number/fax is there on the page. If you are at university think carefully where you might be – hall of residence or flat – if the call comes.

Do spend time and effort over this. Don't be economical when it comes to good quality paper and a decent envelope; find some cardboard as a backing so that your letter does not arrive through the post all scrunched up.

This structure for your letter of application might prove useful.

Paragraph 1

Clarify the post/reference number of job that you are applying for.

Paragraph 2

Give your prospective employer a concise statement of just how you see the post you are applying for. This will be based on your interpretation of the job.

Paragraph 3

Explain concisely and with examples why you think that you can carry out the duties and responsibilities.

Final paragraph

State your feelings about the post. This needs to be crisp and leave the reader with a sense of your commitment and interest in the vacancy.

If you do hand-write this letter then do:

• use decent paper – not small size notepaper
• use black/blue ink or a good quality ink type pen. Remember what we said on pages 98–99, do avoid thin ballpoints because your letter may well be photocopied and such fine writing will all but disappear and with it your chances!

If you word process it or have it done for you by someone else please do check it most carefully for errors. In particular do check to see that you have spelt the title of the organization correctly and that you've got the right name and designation of the person to whom you are writing. It is not a good start to your application if you address it to Mr J Stephens, Personnel Officer, when in fact it should be Mrs J Stevens, Head of Human Resources!

Letter asking for a reference

References are important. You cannot hope to gain a good reference in that it details aspects of your life and work, if the person writing it does not know what you want. It is rude and most unwise to put a name down as your referee and then not tell that person. This will not enhance his or her feelings of goodwill towards you. Besides the issue of politeness comes one of practicality: the referee cannot produce a quality reference if he or she does not know about the position you are applying for and so can tune the reference to match.

You can assist referees by:

• Reminding them who you are and in what capacity you would like them to be a referee (i.e. work, university, personal)
• Providing them with a brief synopsis of the job. You might include a photocopy of the job description.

- Provide reasons why you have requested this person's help for this particular post.

Here is an example:

```
Dear Dr Smith

        Position of Junior Engineer with Ricket and Mann

I was a student at the University 1992-95 and in your
studies advisor groups 1994-5. You also supervised my
final year project on Reliability Problems within Laser
Controlled Optic Devices.

Since leaving University I was with Voluntary Service
Overseas working in India on installation of water pumps
in small villages in North Madras State.

I have now applied for employment with Ricket and Mann
and they have called me for interview on Feb 19th.

I would be most grateful if you could act as my academic
referee. I enclose a copy of the job description plus
some background nature of the organization so that you
can gain an idea of the kind of employment I would have
if successful at interview.

If you feel you would like more information about this
application I can be contacted at 01234-6748 (after 6 in
the evening)

Yours with best wishes
```

Letter of complaint

This is a tricky letter to write. It is often very necessary for yourself and/or the organization you represent. The crucial thing is to establish clearly the facts of the complaint and set those out. Try to follow some kind of logical sequence so that the sequence of the situation you are making the complaint about is readily apparent to your reader.

Activity

Here is an example of a letter of complaint written by a student. What changes would you advise the writer to make?

```
                                      55 South Street
                                         Southport
                                         Merseyside
                                         PR10 4RA

The New Music Club
55 James Sq                             Feb 5th 1996
Bradford
BD 4 6TR

Dear Sir,

   I am writing to complain about the way in which my order
for CDs was delivered to my home address. It was a very
poor service. The paper packaging was torn and when I
opened up the box some of the plastic covers of the CD's
were also damaged.

   Considering all this I am returning the goods as sent. I
would like a replacement or refund.

Yours sincerely

   James Smith
```

You may have spotted the following errors:

- Don't use 'sincerely' with Dear Sir. It should be 'faithfully'.
- If possible find out the name and designation of the person you are writing to rather than use Dear Sir/madam.
- The tone is very cold and abrupt as in *'It was a very poor service'*. There's very little merit in adopting such hostility. The phrase *'I would like a replacement or a refund'* is very blunt.

Compare it to this redraft overleaf. This letter has been improved in a number of ways:

- It is better structured
- The tone is much more acceptable and businesslike. The writer is making his complaint but in a dignified way. At this stage it is not clear who is to blame for the state of the package so there is no point 'coming over too strong'. Remember that as a customer you have a number of protected rights. It is only when these rights have been ignored – as would be the case if this letter was ignored – that a stronger, more insistent tone would be required.

```
                                          55 South Street
                                             Southport
                                             Merseyside
Director of Customer Services                PR10 4RA

The New Music Club
55 James Sq                             Feb 5th 1996
Bradford
BD 4 6TR

Dear Director

          Delivery of CDs. Order No. AB3/196.

   I refer to the delivery of the above order which arrived
on Jan. 29th. Unfortunately the packaging was torn and the
plastic covers round the CDs were broken. In view of this I
am not accepting the goods as paid for.

   I am returning the package and enclosed CDs. I feel that
I am fully within my rights to ask for a refund of postage
(£0.75) and the delivery of CDs as ordered.

Yours sincerely

   James Smith
```

Cultural issues in letter writing

American and British people conducting business in France would normally dispense with formalities on the grounds that they lessen rapport. With both the French, Japanese and to some extent Indians it is important to be sensitive to their formalities of written expression. The business writer to one of these countries would be advised to be rather more formal in phrasing than would be the case with an American or British colleague or boss. Whereas we would sign off our letters with *'Yours sincerely'* or more formally *'Your faithfully,'* in French one would use, *'l'expression de mon consideration distinguee'* (that would be to his or her junior); and *'haute consideration'* (an equal) and *'tres haute consideration'* (to a boss). Even if you are writing in English to your French colleague you would still be advised to start a little more formally than would be the case in the UK. These cultural norms are important to respect.

If writing to an American company is advisable to word process your letter on American size paper (slightly smaller than A4) and use American English spelling – color, center, etc.

See page 209 in the tool box for further information on American English spellings.

Summary

- Letters as well as carrying information do act as PR for you and your organization. That is why it is essential that not only are they well structured, free from ambiguity but also carefully proof-read and checked for accuracy of factual information.
- Letters are designed to be read rapidly. The structure is therefore important. TRAP may help you in this.

  T Topic – setting this firmly at the top of the letter.
  R Response – to the other person's letter, call or fax.
  A Action – what particular action you are to take.
  P a Polite and reassuring close.

- There are all kinds of layouts for letters. Yours will need to conform to a house style.
- It is vital that you consider the tone of the letter and when writing in a letter overseas that you bear in mind that simple direct translation may not be enough.

Further reading

G Ansell and M McMenemy (1985) *English in Business*. Pan Books.
M Cutts and C Maher (1988) *Writing Plain English*. Plain English Campaign.
M Kelcher (1992) *Better Communication Skills for Work*. BBC Publications.

12

The CV and application form

In this chapter we provide advice on putting together your CV. We demonstrate various layouts and provide you with some examples to criticize. We suggest various approaches to the completion of an application form.

CVs

When setting out your CV (curriculum vitae – life's story) do remember that you only have a couple of pages at most. Unless you've had a very boring life so far you will need to be very selective. Here are a few pointers for you to think about when you are preparing your CV:

- Avoid if at all possible producing a general CV. Try and angle it to the organization you are applying to. Avoid the bland and the vague. Making use of a word processor allows you to cut and paste material so that you can have 'on stock' a number of possible versions of the CV. As you career develops so you will be able to cut and paste material from one of your CVs to another for instance:
  - one CV which emphasizes your research record
  - another detailing your work experience overseas
  - one which stresses your record in innovation and managing change
  - another which gives detail as to your management experience, etc.

> ❏ Each CV must be angled towards the needs of the post you are applying for. Do not send a general CV.

- It should be word processed and great care needs to be taken over the structure and layout. Remember it is an exercise in selection.
- Materials must be easy to scan for rapid reading and assimilation of key facts and ideas:
  - use headings not long paragraphs
  - use shortish lines
  - replace long introductions to paragraphs, for example

A) *Since August 1995, I have acted as assistant to a senior partner in the firm of Retort and Bung. Here I have had numerous responsibilities for completing projects centred round new motorway construction and these responsibilities were for budget control of the engineering companies which were subcontracted to the team and who formed an integral part of the project.*

This is printed in 'Zapf chancery' font. It is very dense as a piece of text and is not an easy read with such a lengthy sentence. Compare this with B.

B) Since August 1995, have acted as assistant to senior partner ...
Responsible for completion of ...
Involved in budget control of ...

This is printed in 'Times' font. It is much less dense as a text and reads more crisply. Short phrases replace long rambling sentences.

- Highlight recent work experience but avoid a long list of duties. Bring out your achievements, challenges faced and how you have dealt with them. This is much easier if you've had some work experience and more difficult if you're still at university or college. In that case, think of any clubs, societies, extracurricula activities you have been involved in which can show that you have gained useful and transferable skills.
- Avoid putting together a list of courses attended. Aim to show some kind of logic behind them. Lists seldom convey much information. You have to supply the theme. A list of training courses attended at one level gives information about how many courses you have been to but it could also reveal that you are rather uncertain as to what to be trained for, or that your present job is so undemanding that you keep escaping by going on courses!
- Do think carefully when completing the section on personal interests. This is an opportunity and a very valuable one to show something of you the person – your community, sporting, voluntary involvement. For many people it is the experience that they have gained through their association with sport and voluntary work that has taught them many 'life skills' and developed their characters. Please don't put down a list of bland interests: TV, music, food. What do these tell about you? TV documentaries, Indian cookery and 1970's soul music, they at the very least show some 'flavour'. These flavours can help turn the subsequent interview into more of a conversation.

Transferable skills

It is important that your CV and application form include mention of transferable skills, i.e. those skills that have been sharpened and developed by your time at university and are as it were 'extra' and a bonus to those you have gained as part of your academic course. There have been several surveys to see what it is that employers want from graduates apart from their degree (good ones). The list includes the following.

Communication skills

You can show this on paper by the way your CV/application form is put together.

Problem solving, analytical skills

These are not easy to demonstrate on paper, but mention those situations where you have been involved meeting challenges which require these skills, such as in work placement, problem solving in laboratory experiments, etc.

Team working skills

Here you can mention those occasions where you worked as a key member of a planning group, staff–student liaison committee, sports committee, etc.

Self-management skills

Being able to work under one's own steam, to prioritize work, time manage effectively, etc. There should be instances in the CV where you can highlight the learning that you have done in these areas.

IT and numerical skills

List the programs you are familiar with and the level of competence attained. Don't be vague here.

Language skills

Of increasing importance. Do make mention of any languages you are familiar with and the level of competence – spoken and written – that you have attained. It is always a good idea to include in the CV/application form any time that you have spent working/studying in another country. This shows that you have acquired a certain level of cultural awareness (go easy on describing those summer holidays on Spanish beaches – that does not usually suggest wide cultural education!).

Do be careful not to play the 'CV game'. This is a tendency noted by employers that candidates will blow up work experience, i.e. one week at Marks and Spencers in their food hall selling sandwiches into a whole paragraph on training for management at one of the UK's premier organizations. The problem with this kind of 'puffery' is that sooner or later the player of the game will get found out. One of the key functions of any interview is to check up on claims made in the CV, so stick to the facts.

Here is one employer's view of the CVs he reads.

> 'Most CVs give too much emphasis on the candidates' factual achievements as described by list of qualifications and posts held than the more indefinable personal elements like initiative and character ... I firmly believe personal characteristics are so important in defining the contribution that an individual can make that they outweigh most aspects of experience and training'.
>
> (A. Balfour, Managing Director of Insider Group of Companies. *The Scotsman Newspaper*, 6 November 1995.)

So let's have some of your character and initiatives coming through. This is where the single-page covering letter can help (see page 125).

- Check and double check that you haven't made any spelling, punctuation or grammatical errors. Have someone else check it over for you. Eliminate those small errors which may leave a negative impression: BsC for BSc, driving license (the 's' form is US English), 'my principle (!) reason for taking this course'. Check also that the organization you are applying to does not want you to include a photograph. If that is the case then please don't include some crumpled effort that's been lying around at the bottom of a drawer – the left overs from that passport application you sent last year. It would be a good idea to consider getting some better examples of your impressive mug! Many photo shops offer facilities for head and shoulders shots. The results will be much better than you will get from popping into those booths in your local post office or station.
- Don't go overboard in getting your CV beautifully typed and bound. By all means make sure that it is a very presentable looking document but to have it produced on gold-tinted paper and vellum bound might actually reduce your chances. However, much will depend on the kind of work you are going for. If you are looking outside the world of engineering and more to design and PR, then you can afford to be a little more 'creative' with your approach.

Activity

Here is an example of possible layouts for a CV. Read it carefully and suggest where John Retort could have improved it.

John Retort: CURRICULUM VITAE

Address	**Home**	**Term**
	14 Railway Cuttings	10 Glasgow Ave
	DUMBARTON	COKEVILE
	DN PE 5RA	CE 7 5PR
Tel	Tel 01389-38547	Cokeville 78956

Date of birth 17 Nov 1974   **Nationality** British

Education & 1986-- 1991 Clyde High School
qualifications Standard Grade 6 Credits, 1 General
  Highers Physics B Chemistry B Maths C English C
  1992- 1995 Cokeville University BEng Hons

During my final year I undertook a project to study CAD systems in manufacturing.

Work experience
In my final year at university I gained summer holiday work placement with Brown Bros of Newcastle. I was part of a team that was looking at ways of improving communication with on-site staff. I also made a presentation on my work to employers as part of final year assessment.
During the summer break 1993 I worked for Cokeville Town Engineers Office carrying out work in maintaining office equipment and assisting with orders for new purchases of equipment.

Skills
Driving licence.
Computing Word, Excel. C programming

Interests   Golf: Member of University Team
              University Judo Club member

Referees
Dr H Smith   John Hope
Department of Engineering Director of Special Projects
University of Cokeville   Brown Brothers Engineering
COKETOWN   14 New St
CN6 8TA   NEWCASTLE

Comment

1. Always help your reader, don't make things difficult, i.e. there's no telephone code for Cokeville (suppose someone from the organization you are applying to wanted to phone you at home). Furthermore, there's no indication when the 'home' and 'term' periods start and finish.
2. Avoid vagueness. Think back to that list of transferable skills.
   'I undertook a project to study CAD systems', what does that actually mean in terms of those skills – it could mean a great deal of effort and achievement, team work and analytical skills. Remember, if it's not in the window, the shoppers can't see.
3. There is a general lack of opportunity to sell in the Work experience section.

After reading this we are not that much wiser as to what John Retort actually achieved. *'Improving communication on site'* – this is another of those vague phrases, *'Assisting with orders for new equipment'*. Did he sit copying out invoices or was he on the telephone negotiating with suppliers, keeping detailed records, writing reports on maintenance carried out. All these could be of interest to a prospective employer.

Activity

On the next page is a revised version. Analyse any changes and think carefully of any further developments that you would advise Mr Retort to make.

```
              JOHN RETORT: CURRICULUM VITAE

Address        Home                    Term
               April 5th - May 2nd     May 3rd - June 18th
               14 Railway's Cuttings   10 Glasgow Ave
               DUMBARTON               COKEVILLE
               DN6 5RA                 CE7 5PR

Tel            01389-38547             0112-78956

Date of Birth  17 Nov 1974

Nationality    British

Education &    1986-1991 Clyde High School
Qualifications Standard Grade  6 Credits (English, Maths,
                               Physics, German, Chem, Geog)
               General Grade   (History)
               Higher Grade    Physics B, Chemistry B,
                               Maths C, English C

               1992-1995 Cokeville University BEng 2.1 Hons
```

During my final year at University I undertook a project
with Cokeville Engineers to study their use of CAD in
their manufacturing systems. I included this in my final
BEng project and was invited by the management of the
company to give a presentation at a staff training day.

Work Experience

1993 (5 weeks) Working with Cokeville Town Engineers Office.
Helped in maintenance of equipment and assisted with
placing orders for spare parts, etc. Gained useful
administrative, computing, data handing experience as well
as increased confidence in talking with sales staff and
suppliers.

1994 (6 weeks) Worked with Brown Brothers Engineers of
Newcastle. Part of team assessing communications with on
site staff. Costed out several proposals for mobile
phone/fax and electronic note pads. Tested out
communication systems. Wrote report to management and with
other members of team; made a presentation on results to
on-site-director.

Skills

Communication: As part of my course and during work
experience learnt to give formal presentations to senior
staff; have also written formal reports.
Team work: My work experience has been as part of a team.
Had to keep to strict deadlines and work with much more
experienced staff.
4 years driving experience - clean licence
Familiar with Word, Excel, C++ programming
Basic German

```
Interests
Golf, member of University Team, played in Inter University
matches.
Judo, Captain of University Team. Took part in British
Universities Judo Competitions.
```

```
Referees
Dr H Smith                          John Hope
Reader Dept of Engineering          Director On Site Projects
University of Cokeville             Brown Bros Engineering
Coketown                            14 New St
CN5 4TA                             Newcastle
Tel 01125-75674 Ext 46              N6 4RA
                                    0191-56743 Ext 67
```

Comment

1. There could a little more detail about the nature of his degree course. There is no mention for instance of any electives taken or special subjects studied in final year, etc.
2. He has give a useful description of his work experience. There is a great deal more here than in the first version. He might however, have included other types of work done before 1992.
3. Do we get enough of a flavour of the person from his interests? The word 'captain' has potential for leadership skills. Could he have brought this out a little more?

Overleaf is another layout, perhaps more suitable for those with more work experience.

JOHN RETORT

Address   25 New Drive, London Road
                       BELTON
                       BN4 NT3

Telephone/Fax   01556-56743

Current post   Engineer with Southern Gas Company
                       Responsible for customer service
                       In particular; development of new on-
                       site service teams.

Achievements   Have set up Quality Control Team
                       and led team for successful
                       implementation of ISO 9002.

Previous employment

1979-83: Somerset Gas Company Junior Engineer
Was selected for training on Gas Council Special Scheme
for young engineers. Won GC award for project report.

1983-88: Bridgwater Foundries Ltd Production Engineer
Responsible for development of new CAD systems on shopfloor.
Worked closely with Mercedes Germany to liaise CAD
development.

1988-93: Northern Gas Company Senior Engineer
Assisted in introduction of Investors in People for staff.
Successful award of IIP during my final months with company

Qualifications

BEng Hons 2.2 University of Somerset, 1981
M Eng University of Doncaster, 1987

Skills

Project planning: as in the carrying through of the IIP
scheme with Northern Gas.

Team Work: The enhancement of in service teams at present
employer.

Communication Skills: experienced presenter to groups,
familiar with the production of reports under tight
deadlines.

Full driving licence
First Aid Cert. (St Johns)
Familiar with PCs and software packages, Word and Excel

Interests

Cross country running, member of local athletics club.
Member of local group restoring old steam engines.

```
Date of Birth    Nov 31 1958

Health:          Excellent
Referees

Dr John Nixon              Mr H Jones
Director of Engineering    Chairman
Southern Gas Company       Taunton Athletics Club
Bridgwater House           15 Grove St
Taunton                    Taunton
TN7 5RF                    TN4 8HT

Tel 01345-8974 Ext 67
```

How far do you think John Retort has whetted the interest of a prospective employer. Has he for instance:

- included enough detail about his present job and his previous ones?
- successfully spelt out his achievements?
- provided enough evidence for the skills he lists?
- been wise to ignore his school education? (i.e. is it all a bit remote?)
- been sensible to include his age and health? (what is excellent?)

The supporting letter

This we suggest you enclose with your CV and that it is short, i.e. a single page. In this letter you should:

- Briefly indicate why you are applying.
- State what you can offer by way of skills, experience, etc.
- Draw the reader's attention to **any particular features** of your CV which you think will attract positive opinion for this post.

Activity

Here is an example of such a letter. If you as an employer received it would you be tempted to read the CV with increased interest?

The vacancy is for a junior engineer with experience of on-site communications to join an experienced team. This company has civil engineering projects throughout the UK and is keen to make the best possible use of existing networks. It is anxious to examine the feasibility of satellite communication links.

Personnel Manager
Retort & Bung Chemical Engineers
23 Harrow Way
PRESTON
Lancs
PN5 4TA   Oct 5th 1996

Dear Personnel Manager

              Vacancy for Graduate Recruit (Ref No 67/96/A)

With reference to this application I enclose my current CV.
I would draw your attention to my recent experience with on
site communication systems.

As part of my work I recently toured the US with members
of the team to investigate recent innovations by AT&T and
Bell Telephone Companies. I was provided with a short
placement with Bell Laboratories in Connecticut. This
enabled me to get up to date with some of the latest
satellite led systems.

Over the last three years since graduating from Cokeville
University, I have been part of a team which researched and
installed an on-site information system for Viking
Engineering of Bristol who have sites scattered around the
UK and now throughout France. As a result of my work the
company has secure and highly reliable communications link.
The challenge was great since many of the projects are in
extremely hostile environments.

I am an energetic enthusiastic person with well developed
communication and team working skills. I have the ambition
to become a director of a large company's communication
systems. I am keen to take on further study to assist me
in this.

I look forward to providing you with more information at an
interview.

Yours sincerely

After a careful reading has this letter:

- Provided you with a positive impression of the person?
- Given you some indication that he has the necessary skills, qualifications and experience (enough for you to want to find out more in the CV?)
- Given you a positive impression of the candidate's ability to write a decent letter, free from any spelling, punctuation or grammatical errors, which flows well and makes some coherent sense?

If the answer is **yes** to all these questions then the covering letter has fulfilled its purpose. On the other hand you might have your doubts whether he is overselling himself a little; does he sound a little too eager and ambitious? Or is he the thrusting dynamic type you can't wait to interview?

Apply this kind of criticism to your efforts when you compose such a letter. Remember there's little point in preparing the most superb CV if the covering letter lets you down, it is the first thing to be read. It must create a positive impression.

The application form

If you are still a student you are more likely to be asked to complete an application form than send off a CV. The advantages to a employer of having all the applicants submit a form is that it provides a consistency of approach. CVs as we have seen are very variable in the way they are structured; application forms have already been structured. This means that a large number of forms can be scanned quickly. So

- You must respect the order of the form – don't be tempted to put arrows in to change the pattern of replies. Stick to the boxes provided.
- Complete all sections; don't leave gaps since these can be ambiguous. They can mean that you forgot to write anything or that you failed to see the said box, or that to fill it in might cause some embarrassment to you and perhaps weaken your application in some way.

As soon as the application form arrives through the post, photocopy the original, place it carefully in a drawer inside a plastic cover and get to work on the copied version. By doing this you can make all the mistakes and do all the practise necessary. You will find that application forms do require you to concentrate; they have been put together for a purpose. It is essential that you don't just jump into the application form and start filling up all the boxes.

This form is a test of your ability to read (between the lines), of your ability to write crisply and to the point in the few words that are allowed you.

Remember that this form is going to be read by very busy people – increasingly computers will scan your form and they will be programmed to search for certain key facts such as your qualifications and length of any work experience – so do remember to keep these clearly identified and separated out from the mass of the text.

Always provide a structure to everything that you put down. Go from past to present; work out a chronological ordering of your qualifications and work experiences. Do avoid any arrows directing the readers' attention to some section which has been lost or forgotten from its original position.

We suggest that you word process the form but if that is not possible then do make sure that it is very clearly written. Do use black ink and crisp bold print. This will photocopy well.

In most application forms there is a box – normally half a page sometimes a whole one – in which you are invited to add further details to 'support your application'. Do not ignore this opportunity. It is an invitation for you to 'sell' yourself; for you to provide added value to your application. As with the covering letter to your CV it is an opportunity to stimulate the interest of the readers. Most of the advice relating to the way that you should structure the material in this box is similar to what we have said about CV and covering letters.

Summary

- CVs need to be carefully angled to the particular job you are applying for.
- These must be clearly laid out – the key information must be laid out for rapid assimilation.
- Lists should be avoided, themes are more interesting to read.
- The CV must be carefully checked and proof-read.
- The application form should be completed in full.
- The section 'Further information to support your application' should be completed carefully and in full.

Further reading

J W Davies (1996) *Communication for Engineering Students*. Longman.
C Fletcher (1986) *Face the Interview*. Unwin Paperbacks.
H Dowding and S Boyce (1985) *Getting the Job You Want*. Ward Lock.

13

Note taking, minute writing

In this chapter we provide advice on various methods of taking notes from brain patterns to traditional linear note making systems. We look at approaches to note making from books and at lectures and provide advice for those of you who have to take minutes at meetings.

We've looked briefly at note taking in our chapter on listening. This extends these ideas.

Note taking is an individual business

You will find all kinds of methods for taking notes in the various *How-to Study* manuals on the shelves. What we can do is to suggest a number of ideas you might like to try out; it is very much what you find works for you. Do experiment. See what your colleagues are doing and learn from them. Do try out some of the ideas in this chapter.

Very few people can use shorthand but most of us do have some kind of home made shorthand. You may use arrows and lines, squiggles, and so on, to show yourself what you mean.

More than >   less than <   Increasing ↑   Decreasing ↓

Here are a few points to help guide you in your note taking:

- Never leave your notes too long without writing them up, expanding them and translating all those hieroglyphs (funny squiggles) into English.
- Leave plenty of space between your notes. Be generous with paper. There are several reasons for this. Firstly, you may well need to add more notes to your original jottings; secondly, well spaced out notes look easier on the eye and if you're revising pages of such notes they will be a great deal easier to absorb.

Here is what we mean. Compare page A with page B.

A

Notes are very individual, what works for one person will not suit another. The important thing is to experiment with different systems. Use plenty of space and don't forget to copy out your notes as soon as possible otherwise you'll forget them. Some people go for mind mapping; this can be very helpful

B

<u>Notes</u>
Note takn= v. ind mattr
VIP –exprmt with diff systms
  – use plent space
  – copy out ASAP aftr takng
<u>Mind mappng</u> can be helpfl

We suggest you place the key words as for B on the left-hand margin, then you can add further sub-points alongside, for example

<u>individualistic</u> – many systems – select one to suit – experiment

Mind mapping

This is a system which was made famous by Tony Buzan. We list one of his key books at the end of this chapter. Basically you place the topic in the centre of the page and then group the various sub-themes around it either as they come to you or as you read them from a text. Then follow the sub-themes and you then draw in the links.

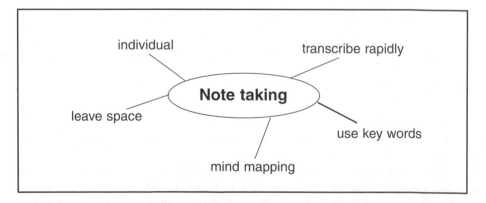

This kind of mapping can be very useful if you are revising a subject. Put the topic in the middle and see just exactly what you remember by jotting down as many points as you can in a wheel pattern. Where the gaps are will be those areas where you may need to do some revision. If it's all gaps, then back to the books!

Shorthand is easier than you think! No we are not talking about real shorthand, but think of this. We recognize words by their shape and it is the consonant that give words their shape. So use consonants and not so many vowels. Look at this:

There is evidence that many engineering firms in UK are not making the best use of the graduates they take on

Eng. fms UK x mkng bst use of grads

Notes can be visual, diagrammatic in form

We looked briefly at learning styles in a previous section (page 5). We saw that some learners find the visual rather than the verbal, written material easier to assimilate. So if it helps you to understand use sketches, maps, diagrams, flow charts even cartoons to supplement your written material. e.g.

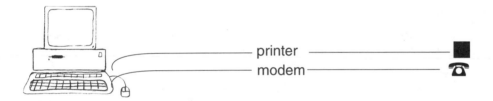

printer

modem

Taking notes from lectures/talks

One of the problems with lectures is that a great deal of information comes at you and unlike having it on a tape you can't press the pause button and catch up with your notes. Assuming you're sitting in a lecture then it will also be very difficult if not impossible for you to ask the lecturer to stop.

You have therefore to find a method of taking notes which will *work for you*. As we've said before do leave plenty of margin space for additional points for follow up discussion, reading, etc. Remember that you will want to use these notes for revision so that it makes sense to make them easy on the eye with regards spacing, the use of plenty of headings and sub-heads.

Some lecturers are very good at providing you with cues as to the structure of the lecture. There will be a number of stages. If you can listen for these it will help you in setting out the headings and sub-heads. What are these stages?

Opening – setting of the topic

'Good morning, today I want to outline some development in quality control within chemical processes.'

Key points

'The key issue is whether despite the development of sophisticated software quality control engineers are able to ...'
 Watch out here for such phrases as:

'Vitally,' ' Of crucial importance'. 'This is important'. 'Please note'. 'You'd be wise to jot this down'. 'Do please remember'. 'Essentially', 'What ever you do don't forget this'. 'Take my advice and consider this carefully'.

Apart from watching out for these phrases, you should also be aware of the body language used by the lecturer when he or she is making these key points. They will usually stress the key words, may be lean forward, point with their fingers, strike the blackboard with the chalk, and so on.

Examples

Watch out for examples, case studies, illustrations used by the speaker. Sometimes these will be very clearly signalled:

'Now I'd like to quote an example from my experience in the RAF', or 'About 10 years ago in the construction of a major oil fired power station ...' or 'I'd now like to illustrate this with reference to what we now know of the Bhopal incident in India'.

At other times the speaker will move into an example without any kind of preamble; you've just got to be quick at recognizing that this shift has occurred.
 These cues are often ignored by students when it comes to note taking. This is a pity, for very often the examples and case studies are really worth noting – even briefly – since they represent 'authentic' professional experiences; they also may assist you in understanding and remembering difficult material.

Summary

This is usually signalled with such phrases as: *'To conclude', 'To sum up'.* It is important that even if you have dozed off during the talk now is the time you should wake up and start writing notes. In the conclusion there will often occur the key elements that you should remember. So listen out for such phrases as:

'So to sum up we've discussed a number of elements which contribute to the development of quality control systems within ...'

This section should be clearly signalled. Most lecturers will try and provide some kind of summary of the key points of the lecture and lead you forward to the next talk.

Some lecturers will provide you with handouts which will in themselves be a summary of what has been said. Our advice would be to add your own notes, comments, underlining, etc. on the handout. There is considerable evidence to suggest that if you remain an active listener you will gain more from a lecture.

To help you remain active, stop you drifting off – especially if the speaker is very slow, the room stuffy or you've a headache – then jot down some questions in the margin of your handout:

• How does this relate to what we had last time?
• What would happen if the ...?
• My experience with the lab work is very different to this, so?

Taking notes from a book, an article, manual, etc.

Firstly, some advice about reading. We're not teaching how to read but you may find that you are having difficulties in reading fast enough or efficiently enough: you find yourself having to reread sentences and taking what seems hours to plough your way through a chapter.

Here are some practical tips to apply:

• Think about your reading as you would changing gear in a car. You need a variety of speeds to be an efficient and effective reader. Many people only have the one – dead slow. This is fine for what we could call *close reading*, where you need to concentrate on every word such as when you are proof-reading your text to spot all the errors. Then there is *very fast reading* skimming through the text. This is where you are trying to gain an overview of what the material is all about. Then in the middle is ordinary paced reading where you know roughly what the text is about and want to get hold of the main points.

So let's run through a reading sequence:

• Pick up the book and just before you open it ask yourself:
• Why am I reading this?
• Who's the author – what's his or her credentials
• When was it written?
• Where was it written US, UK? Does it matter?
• Is there a contents list to get a quick overview of what's included?

- Are there summaries at the each of each chapter or at the end of the text?
- What's it like to read? Dip into a section and see.

When you're sure why you're reading this book (and not just passively drifting into it) then make sure that you have a pad of A4 paper (we would not advise using those shorthand spiral books since they don't provide you with enough space to take good notes).

We would advise the following reading routine:

- A rapid reading of the section/chapter that you've selected – remember you don't necessarily have to start at the beginning, it might be better to start at a point that interests you and which is more applicable. Don't try to read too much at one go. There's little point ploughing on if you are getting tired, the words won't go in; you'll end up by becoming frustrated and starting to dislike the text.
- After the rapid reading go back and take it more slowly; this time start jotting down a few notes. Don't forget that sometimes your notes might take the form of diagrams, sketches, etc.

Your reading environment

Many people find it very difficult to read because they are making it difficult for themselves. There are too many distractions around – too many other things lying on the desk or they are sitting in a bad light, or other kinds of distractions such as a TV set!

If you want to be distracted you'll find something to distract you!

- That half-empty coffee cup saying 'fill me!'.
- Those biscuits crumbs on the plate saying 'let's have another'.
- That unpaid bill lying just on the edge of the desk – saying 'worry over me!'.
- That postcard pinned on the wall in front says – 'I must reply to that invitation!'.

This is why it may be a very good idea to clear your desk, to keep on it only those items that you need for the job in hand. Move away all those potential distractors. Have a clear space in front of you.

Minutes

Minutes are summary points of issues discussed at a meeting.

If you are to take minutes try and see what has been done by others. Try and find out if there is a 'house style' – in other words where the action points are put, if names or initials or designations are used, the amount of detail normally included, etc.

❏ You need to ask other key questions before you write one word for a minute.

Who is to read these?

Are these minutes solely for those who were at the meeting? If so they can be reasonably brief. Are they for those who do not normally attend but like to be kept informed? If so these will need to rather more detailed and some elements of background may well have to be included.

Who should write the minutes?

It is very difficult for a chairperson to take minutes. There is just too much work for the chair to do without having to take minutes. It is best to ask someone who is familiar with the job and feels confident in the role.

What level of detail should be recorded?

How much of the discussion should be minuted? Should it be only a set of bullet points? Should it just record the actions?

Where are the actions recorded?

In the right-hand column? Underneath the discussion?

When are they distributed?

When do you as minutes taker have to have them ready for distribution? When should they arrive on people's desks?

When are the minutes reviewed?

Do members of the group have an opportunity to give feedback to the minutes taker on the way that they are written?

Activity

On the following page are the notes of part of a discussion held at The Faraday University Engineering Department Staff–Student Liaison Committee. Read the rough notes and consider if the minute as written would be acceptable.

Item 3. Blind Marking

Rough notes taken at meeting:

> Fol'ng complnts frm stnds re poss bias in mrkng exam pps wth names attchd discn re ways of introdcg blnd markng system – (no stdnt names on scrpts) practsd   other unis esp US. Vote passd = run pilot schme 1 acd yr witn Dept Chem & Mech Eng. Convnr to write to Hds of Dept

Actual minute:

> Following complaints from students as to possible bias that might be present in the present marking system where candidates' names were used, the committee discussed the introduction of a blind marking system. It was pointed out that other universities, particularly in the US, used such a system and that according to reports there were few problems with it.
>
>   The committee after a vote agreed that a blind marking system should be piloted for one academic year within the Departments of Mechanical and Chemical Engineering.
> **Action:** The Convenor to write to Heads of Department.

It is difficult to comment on this minute since you were not actually present, but you might ask:

* Does it provide enough information?
* Do we need to have more information on 'blind marking'?
* Does it reflect the nature of the discussion – the commitment of the speakers?
* Does the action provide enough guidance for the Chairman?

Style of writing the minutes

There are many different ways of taking minutes. However, they all have the following components:

* They are written in the past tense: *'The chairman replied.' 'The report was accepted.'*
* The passive rather than the active is used, not *'John wrote the report'* but *'the report was written'* (or further back in the past, *'had been written'*). Not *'we all noted the contents of the document'* but, *'the contents were noted'*.

Apart from these there are very wide differences in style and format. Most organizations use some kind of action column. This is normally placed on the right-hand margin and it allows the busy reader to scan down the page to see if his or her name is there and what if any a job is to be done in time for the next meeting!

The active minutes taker

Taking minutes is a difficult job. It is usually one that no one else wants to take on. If you do volunteer remember to be active. You will need to clarify:

- What kind of minutes do you as a group want me to take (detail, length, and so on).
- When do you want them distributed.
- If you should use names, titles/designations, etc.
- Where the actions should be recorded.

> ❏ Try and work closely with your chairman; he or she can be of immense help to you.

- If the chair provides a summary at the end of every item before moving on to the next, this will enable you to jot down notes for the minute.
- If during a very complicated discussion the chair takes a moment to summarize where the discussion has reached then again there's a chance to catch up.
- If there is no summary and you feel that you've completely got lost in the thicket of discussion, then you have a right to say to the group: *'Excuse me, but before we go on could I have some indication of what you would like me to record as a minute?'*

Don't get stuck. Always be prepared to ask your group for their advice. You are there to help them and they should provide you with some assistance of what it is they want recorded.

Summary

- Notes are very much a matter for individuals; there is no perfect model.
- Do experiment with different methods, including brainstorming and using key words. Make use of diagrams.
- Do leave plenty of space between notes and set them out for easy re-reading.
- Never leave it too long before you write up notes – if you do you'll forget what it is you've written.
- As you listen to lectures and talks try and do some mapping – find the key stages. This means being an active listener; listen out for cues.
- When taking notes from a book or article adopt different speeds – fast skim to begin with, then down to slow focused reading – this is when you take notes.
- As minute taker you have a right to clarify your task with your group in terms of what detail they should record, the use of names, etc.

Further reading

S Ashman and A George (1986) *Study and Learn*. Heinemann.
R Barrass (1974) *Study*. Chapman & Hall.
T Buzan (1981) *Use Your Head*. BBC Publications.
J Van Emden (1990) *Handbook of Writing for Engineers*. Macmillan.

14

The report

In this is chapter we examine various approaches to report writing. We provide answers to key questions any report writer needs to ask before commencing and we examine various ways of outlining and structuring the report.

Introduction

Report writing is something that all engineers have to do. It's a fact of their lives. Very few people actually look forward to the writing of a report; it's considered a chore. However, if it is well done it can enhance your own credibility and that of the organization you represent.

Here is some practical advice to help you with this chore so that it becomes more of an opportunity.

If anyone – colleagues, manager, client, etc. asks you to write a report, first *stop* and ask some *questions*. (Refer to the questions we suggest you ask before a meeting, page 83, before giving a presentation, page 67.)

Too many people start blindly writing without asking 'What's this for?' and 'Who is going to read it?'

Here's a list with these and other key questions. Refer to this when someone invites you to write that next report. Many of these questions will also be essential to ask and have answered *before* you start a dissertation or any large project.

- Who's likely to read it – engineers, a mixture of engineers and others, e.g. accountants, designers?
- How much will they know about the subject? Are they experts, novices, or with some experience in the field you are writing in?
- Given the answers to these questions, what exactly are you supposed to cover, i.e. what is your remit?
- Once you are clear as to the remit then ask if there is any special weighting required, i.e. should you concentrate on one particular section more than the others – the quality control issues for instance?
- What is the deadline? Can this be negotiated? Do they want to see a first draft by a certain date and then negotiate the handing in of the final version?

- Has anything similar been written before on this subject by someone in our organization or by someone we could ask, i.e. there's no point in reinventing the wheel.

> ❏ These are the most crucial questions to ask. Never start writing your report – collecting the data – unless you have received reasonably clear answers to them.

Other questions will no doubt come to you, these could include:

- Should this report be written in any particular format (i.e. how the pages are laid out, numbering of paragraphs, etc.) – what is often called the 'house style'.
- Will it require any particular diagrams, graphics? If so, where will I find the relevant materials? Can I access them from my own PC? Will they have to be specially prepared?
- Is the information confidential or copyright?
- Will I need to write an executive summary to accompany this report?
- Will I need to deliver an oral presentation for those who have read the report or to those who have only seen the summary?

There may be other questions. It would certainly repay you to think them through.

Your remit – the terms of reference

Read this example carefully, Do you think this would provide the reader with a clear view of what the report will be about and therefore why he or she should read it?

> To investigate recent failures in lab security and to make recommendations for improvements.

There are a number of problems with this even assuming that the report was written for an internal readership.

- Will the reader understand what is meant by 'recent failures' that is presuming he or she knows about the lab – the particular lab in question and will the term 'improvements' mean much by itself?
- Will I need to make the recommendations at any particular level?

Even if you are writing for an internal readership it's important to mention the key pieces of information. Compare this:

> To investigate failures of security, following two recent thefts (March

3rd and April 9th) of computing equipment from the Kingsway Lab, Department of Civil Engineering and to make recommendations for improvements in security.

Here we have a little more by way of detail, the kind of information that will be useful to many more readers than the first version.

What should therefore be included in any terms of reference/remit at the start of a report?

A reason for writing the report – some idea of intention some notion to whom it is directed.

Readership

As a writer of a report you will hope that your most reports have a fairly similar – homogeneous – readership. However, this is seldom the case; most reports have a mixed readership. What can we do about it?

- Make sure that the terms of reference are clear – as we've seen this will alert your readers and perhaps encourage them to read.
- Make sure that you do not use any more technical, specialist language or terminology than is absolutely necessary so that you don't create any barriers.
- Supply a summary for the 'non-specialist' reader.
- Supply a separate report for these non-specialists.

Let us return to our report on security at the Kingsway Lab. This report may well have at least some of the following as its readers:

- Security officers.
- Managers.
- Members of staff.
- Insurers.

What we have to ask would be the best way to appeal to these different audiences? Much will obviously depend on who are the dominant readers. If we know that of the readers 80% will be in security and 20% in management them we can shape and weight the text and its contents accordingly. We will be saying more about this when we look at structure.

Getting going

Perhaps you suffer from writer's block – this is an inability to get going when faced with a report, essay, dissertation, etc. It's a very familiar problem and one that affects very many writers of all levels. If you do suffer from it then you are in good company. Most writers will experience this 'loss of nerve' and confidence in the writing process.

You can picture the scene. There you are with paper and pen, the deadline getting closer. On the floor beside you a wastepaper basket filled to overflowing with torn up drafts. On the desk an empty coffee cup with the dregs of previous efforts to stimulate the aching brain. The thoughts just won't come. The pen refuses to move. You go back and look through what you've written in this latest draft and are appalled at the many spelling errors, odd seemingly meaningless phrases, etc. You go for more coffee and think of the ever decreasing time limit. Here are some tips to get you out of this block.

Outlining

Having asked the key questions and obtained some answers now is the time to do some outlining. These are the building blocks of the report. Referring back to our Kingsway Lab we could draw up the following outline:

Introduction	Remit
	Brief survey of lab and security systems in operation
Main body	Account of break-ins
	Evidence from similar in other labs in city
Conclusion	What went wrong
Recommendation	Putting it right
Appendix	Technical data

This outline will supply you with the foundations for your report. This is not to say that as you proceed you may not wish to modify the original outline – that's after all what it is, an outline not a rigid structure. But at least it is a starting point.

Having got this broad outline then it's useful to begin to fill it in with more detail. This is the point where your numbering system needs to be thought through, most reports adopt the decimal approach, 1.0, 1.1, 1.12, 1.13, 1.2, 1.21, etc.

Our next level of detail then could appear as:

1 Introduction
1.1 Remit
1.2 Overview of present lab security systems
1.3 Recent changes/improvements made

2 Main body
2.1 Description of break-in – staff
2.2 Police report
2.3 Evidence of similar in other labs in city

3 Conclusion
3.1 Alarm systems
3.2 Staff awareness
3.3 General procedures – induction of new staff

4 Recommendations
4.1 Technical – alarms, etc.
4.2 Staffing and training issue
4.3 Procedural issues

Appendix
1 Plan of labs
2 Outline of present security systems
3 Present documentation for new staff
4 Police and insurance co. figures – similar crimes in city

You see from the above how the outline is becoming more complete, once again we stress it is very much an outline. An important tip: do leave plenty of space between the various points and sub-points so that as you think of perhaps another subsection you will have the space to include it.

Here is an outline from a proposal by an engineering company involved in the oil industry to develop a particular piece of hardware for an overseas client.

1 Introduction
1.1 Executive summary
1.2 Overview or project
1.3 Background to project

2 Hardware development
2.1 End item design and development
2.2 Manufacture
2.3 Factory support equipment
2.4 Maintaining support equipment
2.5 Hardware integration
   2.5.1 Planning and control
      2.5.1.1 Control systems
      2.5.1.2 Control assurance program
   2.5.2 Integration
2.6 Interface development
   2.6.1 Interface control documents
   2.6.2 Operating procedures

As you can see the level of detail can become finer and finer. For those of you contemplating a large-scale production then we would recommend that you do adopt this kind of fine-detailed approach. Remember you may not need all those sub-headings, some may be telescoped together, some may get jettisoned as you proceed, some may get moved into other parts of the document but it is a start.

ABCD headings

When you have worked out your headings you also need to be thinking of the hierarchy they will fall into. It may be helpful to think of it this way:

A   These are your main titles   **18 point bold**

B   2nd headings   **14 point bold**

C   3rd headings   **12 point bold**

D   4th headings   12 point underlined

This pattern is similar to road signs – from main motorway signs to small signposts leading to farm tracks. Your reader will be able to immediately see the hierarchy of signposting; this will help him or her as they skim through your report and its various sub-sections.

Storyboarding

The notion of storyboarding is a form of outlining which we would recommend to you if you are ever engaged on a large project – a final degree thesis, a dissertation, a manual, a large-scale engineering proposal. Basically it is an idea adapted from Hollywood and the film industry. Because camera crews are so expensive you can't have them standing around waiting until you've got the actors ready. They have to know when and where they are going to point their cameras.

A storyboard tells the story of your work. It is like an outline but in more detail; the crucial difference is that the visuals – the graphs, tables, pictures, diagrams, etc., are placed into the 'story' at this planning stage rather than as an afterthought at the end – just bolted on. Figure 14.1 shows what a storyboard could look like.

The story board is a detailed outline with visuals placed in the sequence where they can best complement and support the text. The important factor is flexibility both in the outlining and storyboarding. You might find it useful to use 'posties', you can stick these on large sheets of paper and they can be moved.

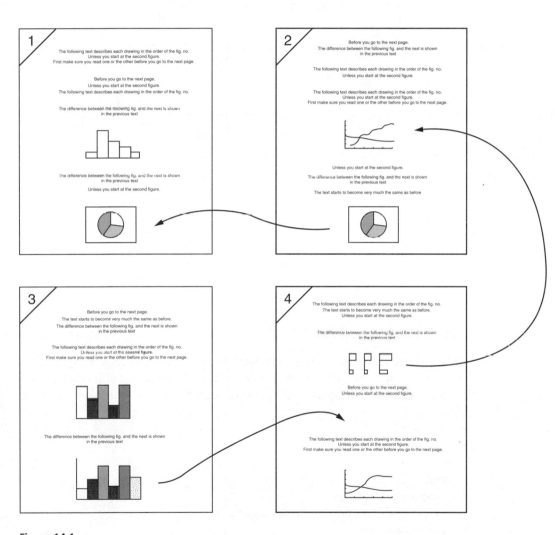

Figure 14.1

Project planning

Producing a report or document of any size will require project planning. Normally you will have a deadline to meet, 'customers' to satisfy, etc., therefore you need to work backwards from that deadline. Here is an example of project planning.

DOCUMENT PROPOSAL

Action point	03/04	10/04	17/04	W/end 24/04	01/05	08/05	15/05
Project approved	✔						
Kick off meeting		✔					
Questionnaires developed			✔				
Questionnaires sent out				✔			
Interviews prepared			✔				
Interviews carried out				✔			
All data analysed					✔		
1st draft report						✔	
Final report submitted							✔

Collecting the data

Having done your outline or storyboard the next step is to collect the data on which you will write the report. There are various methods you can use: the one you select will depend on the kind of report/survey you are working on.

- Questionnaires.
- Observations.
- Interviews.
- Samples.
- Comparative studies.
- Review of documentation and existing data.
- Review of surveys.
- Laboratory tests.
- Off-the-shelf audit/survey packages.
- Fieldwork tests.
- Simulations.
- Modelling systems.
- Logs/diaries.

You will see from the above list which is by no means exhaustive that there are all kinds of methods of collecting your data. You will need to select the one that best fits your purpose.

Hard and soft data

Basically there are two kinds of data you may be collecting as an engineer. Hard data – the quantitative. This considers how many? What numbers? These data are open to statistical and mathematical analysis. These data are concerned with countables, e.g.

- How often did the engine seize up, at what rpm?
- How many students were in the top 10%?
- What percentage of viruses were able to penetrate the computer's protection system?

There will also be occasions when you will need to tap some soft data – the qualitative. This is where you will be asking such questions as:

- What did the staff feel about the new appraisal process?
- Is there a fall-off in morale amongst sub-contractors?
- Do junior staff take health and safety issues seriously?

Such data are more concerned with perceptions and attitudes, with feelings, with experience; it seeks patterns of response. In other words simply to know that 5% of the team do not wear ear-protectors is one thing, but probably of greater interest is to seek to find out why? What are their attitudes (they consider them unmanly, cumbersome, old fashioned, they are made to feel odd; they don't think they will suffer from hearing loss, etc.).

For this kind of question you might make use of the forced choice approach, for example

Q. All those working with heavy machinery should wear ear plugs? (Please tick).

Strongly Agree	Agree	Neither Agree or Disagree	Disagree	Strongly Disagree

The advantage of such questions is that they focus the reader on to the choice and they make the collection and organization of the data (in terms of pie charts, tables, etc.) a great deal easier to display.

There will be many occasions when you will need to collect both quantitative and qualitative data.

Go for it!

When you have produced the outline and the storyboard and you have collected the data you must avoid the tendency towards *writer's block*. As we have said, this is a very nasty disease which can strike without warning and is highly contagious! We suggest that outlining and storyboarding techniques can be of real help to you. Above all we strongly suggest that you ask those important questions concerning why you are writing this report – 'know where you are going' and 'why you are going there?'

The analogy would be if you jumped into a car, started to drive off and then in the middle of heavy traffic you suddenly realized you had no ideas where you were heading or why you were going there!

So you must find out why you are writing this report (or manual or letter) and have some kind of plan or outline to carry you forward as a map will for your journey. Outlining and storyboarding form the essential maps to help you chart your progress, but like your choice of route on a map you can, if conditions permit, change your route, take in a detour, etc. So although outlining and storyboarding are there to guide you treat them very much as guides and not fixtures – immovable that become an obstruction to your progress.

Proof-read before you hand it in

You will find in your tool box at the back of the book various useful tips on proofing your text. Here is an exercise on proof-reading for you to try. The answers are on page 206.

Activity

Proof-read the following text. Remember that the exercise is not just about spotting spelling errors.

Millions Cant Spell Properely

Acording to a survey by Gallup of 1000 adults only one in six adults scored full markes in a test of six familliar words; necessery, accomodation, sincerly,business, separate and height.

Height proved, the easiest word with 84 per cent spelling it correctly while only 27 percent were able to spell accommodation. At least 40 per cent of the women survey got five or more words right compared with just 30 per cent of men. Only 12 per cent of those aged 16- 25 got all 6 words corect while 21 percent of those over 65 years did. So it is dificult to judge wether standards of spelling are improving or not

Case study

A major construction company is alarmed at reported losses of small tools from its several sites around the country. It seeks to carry out a survey to find out the extent of the problem and what can be done to reduce the thefts. Before detailing the exact remit, a small group brainstorm the following questions. Note, not all questions raised by such methods will necessarily go into the remit; they are starting points for the report.

What questions would you have raised in such a brainstorm?

- Is the theft caused by breaks-in and vandalism?
- Is there evidence that any of our own staff are responsible?
- Does most of the theft happen during working hours?
- What particular equipment is stolen, is there a pattern?
- Are there any seasonal factors at work?
- Are the patterns of theft similar right across the country – are there regional factors at work?
- How does the firm compare with our competitors in this matter of theft?
- How do last year's figures compare with previous ones?

From these questions will emerge a possible remit.

To investigate the current spate of thefts of small tools from company sites across the country; to determine whether there are any particular features or trends and to determine what measure the firm should use to reduce this problem.

Activity

Overleaf is the actual report that was written. Read it carefully. Decide what changes you would wish to make to improve it.

Dig AHole Contraction PlC
Report on Loss of Small Tools from sites

Author: C H Isel

Date: Dec 3rd 1996

To: Director of Purchasing

1Remit

This is report is the outcome of a survey carried out by
the author following a proposal by the Director of
Purchasing to investigate:
The extent of thefts of small tools from company sites
The nature of these thefts
What measures the company might adopt to reduce the
problem.

2.Background

The annual bill for the loss of equipment from construction
sites across the UK is estimated at around £500m or about
1% of the construction industry's total turnover. During
the last three years the problem has been given much more
publicity. The Home Office have recently set up a Plant
Theft Action Group. This body comprises manufacturers,
hirers and insurers and is working on measures to combat
the massive problem of theft in the construction industry.
Small tools are part of this problem. In 1992 the company
calculated that we were losing some £8000 per month through
the theft of small tools from its construction sites.
From evidence given by site managers this figure would
appear to be an underestimate and that we could be looking
at loses at some £12000 per month.

3Method

A meeting was held in Nov.1995 of site managers; it was
proposed that a survey be undertaken to ascertain the exact
nature of the problem and to draw up an action plan for
prevention of theft. 10 sites were visited and other sites
were sent questionnaires. During the visits, security
systems were checked and records of thefts analysed. Some
local police forces were spoken to and discussions were
held with The Home Office.

3Findings

In general the problem is more serious that had been
estimated. Most sites do suffer continual losses of small
tools. Site Managers are becoming almost resigned to this
fact. The survey found that:

1. The small tools most often stolen were: hammers,
chisels, and screwdrivers
2. All sites were affected. There appears to be little
difference whether the site is situated in a small town or
large cities. There appear to no regional variations.

3. The winter months Dec- March appear to be the highest for losses; it might be that the early nights may assist thieves.

4. Although vandalism is a problem there did not appear to be much of a connection between acts of vandalism and this theft.

5. Site managers were naturally cautious over the question whether their own staff were responsible for the thefts. However in answers to the questionnaires it was apparent that some managers and staff saw this as a problem. It appears that amongst a small minority of staff taking is considered as 'borrowing'. This is almost regarded as a 'natural right' and a perk for the job. Such staff according to the evidence we came across do not see these 'borrowings' as theft.

6. Anti theft measures were applied inconsistently across the sites. Of the 10 which were visited only 2 had applied in full the security measures recommended. There were instances of:
- failures to keep accurate records of purchase of small tools
- small tools having no company mark on them
- tools rooms left unlocked
-little or no attempt to collect up small tools at the end of the working day.

7.1 A reluctance by some site managers to talk to staff frankly about this problem. There was a feeling that it was better to let sleeping dogs lie. This attitude is tied up with the view that taking tools from the site equals 'borrowing'.

6 Conclusions

This investigation has established that there is a serious problem with regard to the theft of small tools. Our calculation is that over £15000 worth of such tools is being lost to the company. This is a serious waste of money. Furthermore we had evidence from the questionnaires and the visits to sites that such losses had an impact on good time keeping (staff going in search of spare tools, having to make use of older tools because new ones were missing etc.). We were told of one instance where a site foreman's life had been endangered because the bolts that should have been tightened on a lifting platform and had not been done sufficiently thoroughly because no spanner could be found (they had all been stolen) so resort had to be made to one carried in the boot of the manager's car - this did not fit properly hence the lucky escape.

From this incident all tools should be recorded in and out by a supervisor each working day.

7.Recommendations

We recommend as a result of this survey that the following actions are put in place:

1. Site managers should be written to. A copy of this report should be sent together with a strong reminder that Memo S/91/95 be acted upon without delay. In particular:

2. Site managers to keep accurate records of losses and purchases to renew stocks

3. Small tools to be collected at the end of the working day and locked away

4. All small tools to be marked in an appropriate way so as to identify them as company property

2. A letter from the Director of Purchasing to be written to all staff providing them with the essential conclusions from this survey and a reminder that thefts of small tools- borrowings- is strictly against the company's code of discipline. Strong action leading to dismissal will be taken.

3. We investigated various security systems currently on the market and do not see their use as being very practical on sites.

Note: We discussed our problems with the Head of Security in E15 a business unit of John Mole Construction who operate in similar locations to ourselves.

They have managed through good housekeeping, strict audit and accountability to reduce in the last two years their losses of small tools by 72%.

Signed................................

Comment

There are a number of problems with this report. Did you spot some or all of them?

1. Numbering system is haphazard – two number 3s. Why 3.7.1 if there is no 3.7.2?
2. A discrepancy in the figures quoted – losses of £12,000 per month are mentioned in the background section but £15,000 in the conclusion.
3. There is a discrepancy between the remit provided to the author and the one he quotes in this report. Where is there any mention of 'any particular features or trends'?
4. Under Method, this report does not make clear what were the criteria for selecting the 10 sites, i.e. are they a sample?
5. There is no reference to the questionnaires elsewhere in this report, has the author forgotten all about them?
6. Note the phrase 'Some local forces'. What was the rationale behind this 'some'?
7. Findings section. A report writer needs to be very careful with such phrases as: 'It might be that the early nights may assist thieves'. Is this information provided by site managers, from observations, from police files, etc.?
8. Conclusions. Is this the place for the material on the site foreman's life being endangered? Is this not a finding?
9. 'All tools should be recorded'. Is this not a recommendation and therefore should not be in this section. This section is very closely printed. It would be much easier to read if the text were better spaced out.
10. Recommendations. There has been no previous reference to Memo S/91/95. We must presume that this document is referred to earlier in Finding No 6 as 'the security measure recommended'.
11. There is a vagueness in the phrase, 'all tools should be marked in a appropriate way'. Should there not be some company standard mentioned here?
12. Is the Note written at the end of the report the best place for this material? Perhaps this section might have come in an appendix with some more detail as to how this company actually operated its new systems.

So, as you can see, there is considerable scope for improving this report. Report writing is a difficult business. We strongly recommend the texts we list at the end of this chapter.

Summary

- There is little point in sitting down to write a report unless you have received a clear remit as to what should be covered.
- You need to know what kind of readership you will be writing for.
- Consider some form of outlining and storyboarding as a map to guide you in the writing of the report.
- Think carefully about your ABCD headings and the logic behind the arrangement of these.
- Remember that report writing is a form of project planning. You will need to work backwards from the actual delivery of the report so that you can collect the necessary data and write the preliminary drafts.
- Do make sure that you proof-read your report before you hand it in. Do not trust everything to the spell checker.

Further reading

C Turk and J Kirkman (1982) *Effective Writing*. E & F N Spon.
J Van Emden and J Eastal (1993) *Report Writing*. McGraw-Hill.
G Wainwright (1987) *Report Writing*. Management Update.

15

The lab report

We take you through the various sections of a typical lab report that most students of engineering are asked to complete during their courses. We examine the layout and structure and provide you with some advice on style.

The aim of a practical lab class is for you to put your theoretical knowledge into practice. It also aims to train you to observe the results of any work done and thirdly to encourage you to practise your communication skills in the reporting of results and conclusions. This reporting is usually carried out in the form of a written report. It is this that we examine here.

Style

Lab reports are almost invariably written in the passive and in the third person (for more details of active and passive consult the tool box on page 214). Basically the difference is one of focus.

I fastened the twin hoses to the regulators.

This is an active sentence and the focus falls very firmly on I the author, the person who carried out the experiment. However, we the readers are usually more interested in what was *actually done* rather than who did it, so the passive is used;

The twin hoses were fastened to the regulators.

Do try to avoid unnecessary and clumsy passive expressions as in:

- It was noted that temperature rose rapidly.
- It was observed that.
- It was seen that, and so on.

Simply write: The temperature rose at a rate of ..., etc.

Structure

This will depend on the 'house style' set by the department you are in. Some set very firm guidelines, others favour a more flexible approach. Do be sure to find out what are the 'house' rules before you start!

Here are a few sub-headings for you to consider.

Title

This as in all titles needs to be specific, e.g.

An experiment to test the relationship between resistance and temperature in a copper wire.

Aims of investigations

The various aims need to be set out clearly and in order of procedure.

1. To examine the construction of a three-phase squirrel cage motor.
2. To study the no-load and full-load characteristics of the motor.

Theory considered

Here is an example

According to kinetic theory, a temperature rise increases the kinetic energy of the atoms and makes them vibrate more vigorously. The electrons moving through the conductor will experience more violent and frequent collisions, so that the electron flow increases. The change in resistivity for semi-conductors is due to a change in the number of free electrons; these increase with the rise in temperature. This experiment is designed to test the nature of that change in resistivity.

Apparatus/equipment used

Some house styles insist on 'Equipment' or 'Experimental' as titles. You may well be asked to provide more than just a simple list of equipment used: drawings, diagrams, etc.

Remember that your aim here is to provide illustration as to how a piece of equipment worked in your experiment. You will not be asked for a detailed drawing of what it looks like. Keep the drawings simple; focus on the parts which most concern you. The key test is: could someone else repeat your experiment using your equipment? If they couldn't then you have not made it clear enough what equipment you used or how you used it.

Precautions and safety issues

Greater emphasis is now given to this section. Many students do not take this very seriously and just trot out a few phrases about all trailing wires to be removed; surfaces to be kept clean; goggles to be worn, etc. Avoid this kind of bland writing:

> Slippery floors are dangerous. Oil spills from machines do occur. Non-slip shoes must be worn.

Try to think through the likelihood of a hazard, write the precautions taken in such a way that any reader can appreciate your motive, for example

> Oil spills from the machines are very difficult to eliminate entirely. The vibrations caused will inevitably cause some oil to drip. Trays can be placed under the machines, but there is always some chance that oil will reach the floor. Non-slip shoes will prevent accidents. They should be worn at all times near the machinery.

Procedure/methods employed in tests

This sets out the order, the logical pathway that was followed in order to conduct the experiment. Again the acid test is: could someone else following these steps get a similar result?
   This section sets out in order the procedure that was used.

> The oxygen and acetylene cylinders were secured to the base. The oxygen cylinder was opened slightly in order to remove any dust present. This step was repeated with the valve which was opened slowly using a T-handled wrench.

Results obtained

These need to be set out clearly as in:

> The moment of inertia was found from the experimental values for a steel wheel and axle assembly. This is calculated to be 0.4207 kg m^2. when compared to the standard value which is 0.4386 kg m^2. There is an experimental error of 4%. This may have been due to incorrect measurement.

Analysis of these results

This is a crucial part of any lab report. It is one thing to get the results it is quite another to be able to interpret these. This section will often make the difference between those that get As and Bs. If the results did not work out as expected why was that? If they did are there any further thoughts that might be useful to record.

An engineer should always be on the look out for reasons why things work and why they don't. You never know but that small discrepancy that you noted could be the start of something very interesting. After all it was a small change in a mould on a glass slide which first alerted Fleming to the possibility of penicillin.

Tutors marking these reports wish to see that you have been doing some thinking, some analysing, some hypothesizing. If readings don't come out as expected then you will need to analyse why. If there are alternatives to the interpretation of a result, then you should state some of the possibilities. Avoid blaming the vague, all embracing phrase: human error. Do try and discover where the error occurred.

As an apprentice engineer so to speak, you need to train yourself to spot errors and if they do occur then you need to show that you can analyse the probable reasons for their occurrence. Do be as precise as you can. Avoid vague terms such as, *approximately* or *reasonable agreement*. Here is an example of a student writing her analysis section:

> In the first part of the experiment the transmission factor being below 1 suggests that some light did not pass through the glass block. This may have been due to the reflection of absorption of light by the glass itself. On the other hand the blocks although being carefully lined up may have had gaps in them; these were not taken into consideration in the calculations. These may have caused the readings to be inaccurate. Alternatively ...

Note how the student is thinking on paper. It is crucial that you try to analyse any errors that occur in the results you obtain. It is by so doing that you may learn a great deal about your methods and the difficulties that can occur when performing any measurement. Error analysis will encourage you in critical thinking. Remember the failure to spot a small error can have major consequences:

> The failure of the Russian Mars 96 probe in November 1996 appears to have been caused by a simple mechanism consisting of four latches and a spring which linked Mars 96 to the booster. It was a mundane basic thing which perhaps was not greased properly. But on that small error £180 million was wasted and the hopes of many scientists dashed.

Performing rigorous error analyses will provide evidence to your prospective employer in your CV and application form to support your claim that you possess problem-solving skills! So hone them up in the lab and when you write them in the reports.

Conclusions/discussion section

Remember that at the start of the report you stated an aim. The conclusions should relate to this aim and how far you managed to achieve this.

> The amount of calcium carbonate in sample x was found to be between 18.97 g/100 g and 20.08 g/100 g. It can be concluded that the determination of $CaCO_3$ by volumetric analysis is not a reliable method as the result is inaccurate. This method cannot be used when accuracy is vital.

A lab report is then designed to show that:

- you have understood the brief
- you have thought through the methods carefully
- you have related the experiment to the theory you have been taught
- you have assembled equipment in a logical and thorough fashion
- you have demonstrated by your actions that you are aware of safety
- issues and have conducted the experiment accordingly
- you have carefully and systematically noted the results of the work
- you have discussed any results in a way that shows that you are thinking through the implications
- you have made an attempt to draw out conclusions in a way that demonstrates that you reflected on your work.

In the introduction to this book we mentioned different kinds of learning. If you can get into the habit of *reflecting* on success and failures you will be taking those steps to continuous development and life-long learning. Lab reports may appear to you as a chore, another assessment hurdle to pass through. Try and see them as a way of sharpening your abilities to analyse, interpret and communicate your conclusions. These are all skills that are highly transferable in any branch of engineering and at any level of work.

Summary

- Find out if there is a house style for writing the report and stick to it.
- Do not use the first person (I) but also do avoid long-winded passive expressions (e.g. 'it was noted').
- Take great care not to be vague.
- Analyse in a logical and orderly way. Remember that if the experiment does not turn out as expected this may afford you valuable opportunities to reflect on any discrepancy. The 'failure' might be more interesting and valuable than the 'success' that is provided that you analyse the reasons why.

Further reading

J Van Emden (1990) *A Handbook of Writing for Engineers*. Macmillan.

16

Writing a specification

In this chapter we look at key criteria for writing specifications. These include: accuracy, consistency, conciseness and clarity of expression. We offer advice when editing or translating a specification.

Definition

A specification specifies! It sets out the criteria for the constituents, conditions, operation, performance, reliability, maintainability of an equipment or part of an equipment.

> The hazard lights will operate when the button on the dashboard is pushed in; they will operate for 30 seconds only unless the button is activated to its secondary position.

Just imagine you have hired a car for the day and it has broken down on the motorway. You pull in to the hard shoulder and push the hazard warning lights button. You notice that after a moment they stop working. You push the button again. Thankfully the lights start flashing, but to your extreme annoyance and frustration they stop again. You believe this to be a fault of the equipment, so you keep on pushing until finally you consult the manual in the glove pocket and read the above 'specification'. You are still not much wiser. 'Activated to its secondary position' is still vague. A better description might have been:

> To operate the hazard lights, push button marked HAZARD on the dashboard.

> This will activate front and rear lights on the car for 30 seconds.

> If you want these lights to remain flashing for longer than 30 seconds, then having pushed the button in, move it to the left until you hear a click. The lights will remain flashing until such time that you push the button in again.

This is a much better description but it is not a specification; it does not set out the limits of operation, for instance:

remain flashing – how often? With what intensity (i.e. when is a flash not a flash but a twinkle!)

move it to the left – how far, are we talking of centimetres or millimetres (or even inches?).

It is only when we start writing a clear description and then start thinking through the boundaries of operation that we discover (a) just how very difficult the writing of a specification is and (b) just how very necessary it is to do it well if someone is going to operate the article in question safely and efficiently.

> ❏ A specification spells out the obvious. Remember what is obvious to you may not be to your reader!

> ❏ The writing of clear specifications is of increasing importance as quality issues become central to the work of all engineers.

Companies seeking to move to international standards of quality (ISO 9002) must provide specifications for all their operations and components. These must be written clearly. There must be no puzzlement or guessing when it comes to these being read.

Key aspects

Accuracy

The specification must describe the component. In a sense all engineering is approximate but the variance, plus or minus, must be specified; this is important when it comes to size, weight, constituents, tolerances, materials used, etc. It is no use being vague. That will not do.

Conciseness

Specifications are written on the basis that a certain amount of technical experience and familiarity on the reader's behalf can be assumed. Long-winded explanations must be avoided. If there is any doubt that a term used will not be familiar to your reader, then you must gloss (explain) the term and provide a glossary of terms as part of the documentation. The glossary is normally placed at the beginning of your list of specifications. This should alert your reader to terms he or she will be meeting.

Clarity

In our section on this in your tool box, pages 212–214, we deal with issues of ambiguity. In the writing of specifications there must be nothing left unclear or potentially ambiguous. Just consider the difficulties and dangers that would result if the person(s) reading the specification construed another meaning rather than the intended one.

> Control panels and control valves are supplied; they are activated in the case of the temperature exceeding 30°C.

Which are activated? The panels or the valves? Now to be fair the context in which the sentence is written will usually supply the meaning but we should not rely on this. Each sentence should be as clear and unambiguous as possible.

Consider this specification:

> The 10 V dc supply line shall have a return line separated from the supply line.

This sounds reasonably clear. But consider could this mean:

> The return line for the 10 V dc supply shall be separate from all other 10 V dc lines?

or

> The 10 V dc supply shall have dedicated return line but other dc supplies may share a common return line?

As with all specifications the important thing is, as we have said so many times before, is: *'Know your audience. Put yourself in their shoes.'*

Ask yourself: is there more than one possible interpretation? Test out your drafts on others. Can they see any ambiguity in the phrasing? Is there any looseness in the wording?

Consistency

Readers will need to be reassured that there is consistency of approach in the writing of the specifications. It will not do much for this reassurance to see HD written for hard disk on page 1 and Hd Dk written for the same thing on page 2, not to mention Hard Dk on page 5 and even HARD DISK on the final page!

Currency of specification: the sell-by date!

There must be a very clear indication as the currency of the specification, for instance if it is a replacement for an older one – the 1996 specification which differs from that written in 1995. There must be a clear indication that previous specifications do not apply as from a certain date. This must be written into the manual or procedural document.

> **All** specifications listed in handbook 97 are to be replaced by those marked 98. Specifications listed under vol. 97 will **not apply** from Jan 1st 1998.

Structured

A specification should always seek to lay out for the reader the structure that the operation shall follow; the logic behind any sequence, a pathway that the reader can pursue. This is very important when it comes to a staged sequence of any kind.

Activity

Have a look at this specification from electrical engineering. This addresses many of the points we have covered. How would you improve it?

Specification 145 Laser Safety

The Cable, Interlocks, shall ensure that the laser fired torpedo cannot be launched unless all hatches and safety covers are closed or in position and that the correct items of optical test equipment are fitted in to the laser beam path by providing a 28V signal to the RN Launcher only when all interlocks are made.

Comment

For a start the sentence is far too long and awkward to read. The structure is not obvious. What we need are answers to the questions:

- What is it?
- What does it indicate?
- How does it ensure safety?

Compare this version:

Specification 145 (96) Torpedo Launch Safety

The cable, INTERLOCKS, shall provide a + 28V dc signal to the RN Launcher to indicate that all safety covers are in position and all hatches are closed.

This signal shall indicate that the correct items of optical test equipment are fitted into the laser beam path.

The torpedo cannot be fired unless this signal is present.

This provides a much better specification in the fact that it is clear and easy to follow. Here is an example of a design specification:

```
                    Design Specification

This document should be a clear technical manual. The main
aim is to provide enough information so that a list of
tests can be drawn up that will give 100% confidence in its
function.

1) DESCRIPTION: A clear description of the basic function
of the unit, history of its development and how it will
integrate into a higher assembly.

2) TECHNICAL REQUIREMENTS: The unit should function to a
specific standard as determined by the designer. All
parameters and limitations of the design must be presented
at this stage. This will ultimately become the source
reference document,

e.g., with an input of + 5 Volts at pin 5 the output shall
be a 5 KHz Square wave

With an instruction of the form above, test equipment can
be developed and supplied so as to provide the necessary
input and record the outputs accurately.
```

Editing and translation – particular caution

Whenever you edit a text you run the risk of altering its intended meaning. Even a word removed can make a difference, a comma removed as we will see in the tool box on pages 209–210 can alter the sense quite radically.

If you are going to edit a specification then you must go back to the author – the engineer in question – and seek his or her views on what to do.

The same degree of caution is necessary whenever a specification is translated. If you have ever studied a language you will know even in a most elementary fashion that it is not simply a matter translating one word or phrase for another, the sense has to be translated.

The celebrated use of the word **ignore** used by the Japanese after the US government had offered them surrender terms following the bombing of Hiroshima has been analysed as actually having meant: 'Decision Deferred' which is rather a different proposition from 'Ignore' and one that, as the history books relate, had tragic consequences.

When working on a translation of a specification – or for that matter any technical writing – test out the translation if at all possible on a native speaker/user of the language. Ask him or her if the sense is the same as the intended meaning. Computer programs which instantly translate your English text into Japanese will no doubt be accurate in strict grammatical and vocabulary terms but you need to know if the precise sense is carried across.

At a simple level your computer will tell you that the French for deep is *profond* but that does not mean profound in our sense of the word – i.e. deep in thought. You can easily get into deep waters. Take care!

Summary

- Specifications are there to specify. To do this well they must be accurate, 100% clear and concise.
- Test out any specification on others to see if there are any hidden ambiguities.
- Be exceptionally careful when you are editing or translating a specification.

Further reading

V Summers (1991) *Clear English*. Penguin.
J Van Emden (1990) *A Handbook of Writing for Engineers*. Macmillan.

17

Proposal writing

In this chapter we offer advice as to how to put a proposal together; the principal criteria to bear in mind when drafting a proposal and the importance of relating any proposal to the specific needs of your customer.

Definition

A proposal is a selling document. It attempts to sell an idea and therefore to win business for your team, department or organization, usually against others.

Although a proposal is about selling an idea, a piece of equipment, a process, etc., it must persuade the reader with facts and logic. It will not do this if it is all puff and no substance.

A proposal is an offer. It could be in response to an offer outlined in the Ministry of Defence Contracts Bulletin; this is distributed widely on a fortnightly basis and lists all the various proposals that the MoD is interested in. For example:

Proposals Invited
CRB1b/1249 Overhaul of Rotating Electrical Assemblies fitted to military wheeled vehicles.

A proposal is a response to a customer's needs and whether that customer is the MoD or your local school or factory these needs must always be kept firmly in mind. They will usually come in written form and will indicate:

'Our organization has some specific needs that we cannot meet. We would like your organization to make us an offer as to how you can fulfil these. In order to appraise your offer we would like from you a proposal which will include:

- Your qualifications for the job – staff profiles and CVs.
- Your track record in performing similar work.
- Your quality control systems.
- Your costs.
- Your ability to keep to deadlines.
- Any other details relating to the proposal that you feel we should know.'

There will be many other questions, but unless the organization receives reassuring news on these then it is not much point going further with the relationship. Naturally a proposal has the best chance of 'winning' if it closely matches the customer's needs, if the price seems reasonable, if the product can be delivered on time and if the track record for this kind of work stands up to scrutiny. If these are met, then your organization stands a chance of winning the business. In other words it is *compliant*.

If for any reasons the proposal that you write (either individually or as part of a team) is *not compliant* then the reasons for this must be clearly spelled out. You must be able to persuade the reader that your reasons are acceptable and can be justified. For example: *we have a cheaper/more efficient solution.*

It may be that your solution is different and better in terms of efficiency. Remember, however, that no one likes to be told by a potential provider that he/she has got it wrong. This is where you have to be diplomatic. Information supplied by the US Navy as to why proposals submitted to them over the period 1980–7 were not successful included the following:

- Oversimplification of technical requirements.
- Failure to address technical requirements.
- Misinterpretation of specifications.
- Failure to offer convincing details as to costings.
- Failure to provide sufficient reassurance as far as meeting deadlines were concerned.

Bid/no bid decision

When an offer to write a proposal arrives (this could be as a result of a meeting, conference, response to a prospectus, etc.) then it is time to decide whether your organization will decide to go to the trouble, time and cost in developing a proposal.

A meeting of the key participants who will be involved is necessary. It is helpful if they have already received any preliminary papers relating to the proposal. This meeting is to decide whether it would be feasible to go ahead remembering that a fully prepared and costed proposal could cost many hundreds or thousands of pounds. Here are some of the key questions that would need to be asked at such a meeting:

- Have we anything which with *minor* adjustments could be used?
- Do we have anything which with *major modifications* could be used?
- Would it be worthwhile undertaking a great deal of *new work* in order to be in a position to win this business, i.e. how badly do we need this given the likely costs and profits?
- Would this new business help us in our long term? Is it a one-off or could we look to repeat contracts?

You will remember that in our chapter on report writing (pages 139–154) we looked at project planning. These techniques are even more important when it comes to the preparation of such a major document as a proposal. Keeping to deadlines will be crucial. A project management outline could be along these lines:

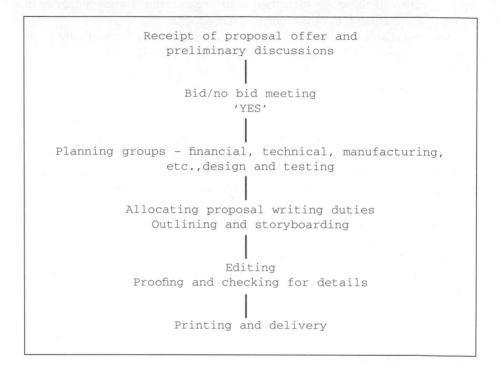

```
              Receipt of proposal offer and
                 preliminary discussions
                           |
                  Bid/no bid meeting
                        'YES'
                           |
  Planning groups - financial, technical, manufacturing,
                etc.,design and testing
                           |
           Allocating proposal writing duties
              Outlining and storyboarding
                           |
                        Editing
            Proofing and checking for details
                           |
                 Printing and delivery
```

Persuading your customer

In writing the proposal you will need to perform a kind of modified SWOT analysis: Strengths, Weakness, Opportunities and Threats, by answering these questions:

Why us?

What have we got going for us to help win this bid?
Where do we score? How can we play on our assets?
How much will the customer know about us?
Do we need to correct any misinformation that our would-be customer may have?

Why not us?

What are our deficits? How can we circumvent these? How can we turn a seeming deficit into a strength or opportunity (i.e. we are a small organization, but we can be flexible and rapid in meeting your requirements; we don't have any cumbersome bureaucracy to slow us down!).

Why another?

Who are our likely competitors? Can we assess their relative strengths against us? How can we gear our proposal so as to minimize their relative strengths and maximize ours?

Themes in the writing of a proposal

We want our readers to be aware of certain broad themes as they read our document. These are the keys that will help to unlock any doubts and establish our credibility as to why we should be selected. As they are key themes we must make certain that they are appropriate for our purpose and that they are repeated with conviction. Such themes could include:

- Our approach is evolutionary; we build successfully on previous work and by so doing we ensure low risk.
- Our engineering excellence is proven; we have an experienced systems team enhanced by subject specialists.
- We are committed to quality. You are welcome to inspect our procedures.
- We are a small flexible operation and can react with speed to situations; our track record demonstrates this ability.
- We consistently meet deadlines

Who will assess our proposals?

It is vital that we consider very carefully the likely readership for our work. We went through a number of key questions on audience when dealing with reports (page 141). These are all relevant. In addition we should plan the writing so that the reader will understand.

The non-expert reader

Senior management should get a management summary and a systems summary. This will provide them with a good overview of the proposal without, in any part, going into too much depth.

The expert reader

The technical experts, the build and design authorities, get a systems summary together with a detailed technical/design breakdown.

The financial reader

The customer's accountants may get the management summary and systems summary, but certainly detailed financial information.

The legal expert

The customer's lawyers get the management summary, the systems summary, a summary of costings and detail on all aspects of the contract, particularly those relating to the penalty clauses, etc.

If you are reading this as a student then much of what we are suggesting may seem rather remote for your needs. However, it is just as well to familiarize yourself with what is an essential part of the engineering business. Proposals lead to work. Well written and well thought out proposals that answer customers' needs help win that business. We have constantly stressed in this book the need to *'know your audience'*. Nowhere is this advice more essential than in proposal writing. If you do not know what your customer wants then it is very unlikely that you will be able to satisfy these needs through any proposal and so vital business will be lost.

Summary

- Read very carefully what your customer wants. Aim to be as fully compliant with these needs as possible.
- Proposal writing to be successful – that is to win business – must constantly address customers' wishes and needs.
- Where you cannot be compliant then you must spell out your reasons clearly.

Further reading

H Silver (1992) *Writing Winning Proposals*. McGraw-Hill.

18

Graphical communication

In this chapter we look at some of the key reasons why we would use graphics to communicate our written and presentation information to our readers and audiences. We look at some of the advantages of using graphics and some of the problems encountered. We provide you with examples of the use of various graphics and invite you to consider their advantages and disadvantages.

Introduction

Graphical communication refers to the use of tables, pictures, diagrams, maps, histograms, pie charts, x and y graphs, flow diagrams, etc., in fact every possible visual approach to the conveying of information. In this chapter we are looking at the use of visuals both in written texts such as reports and manuals, and in oral presentations where overhead slides, 35 mm pictures and presentation programs are increasingly used.

You've probably heard the expression, 'A picture is worth 1000 words'. There is a great deal of truth in this; the trouble is that it has become rather a meaningless phrase. It implies that there is some special worth in visuals as against words. You may have seen various forms of graphical representation being used which only serve to add a bit of glamour to an otherwise dull text. There is always the risk of swamping your reader or listener with graphics.

Let us say at the outset that graphics can be extremely useful and at times absolutely essential. Can you imagine explaining company accounts without the use of tables and charts, or progress reports on engineering projects without flow charts and graphs? However, this acknowledgement of the desirable nature of graphics should not hide the fact that they can be easily misused, sometimes intentionally but more often than not through ignorance or carelessness.

Some general hints

Ask yourself:

• Why am I using this graphic?

- Do I understood the graphic and the information it contains?
- Will my audience understand the graphic?

To help you answer these questions, it is often a good idea before you get into elaborate work on your computer to do some experimenting with pencil and paper. Try out various possibilities. Certainly do a trial run of your graphics if possible with a few of the audience who will be reading or watching the graphics. This might give you some very useful feedback. Remember in our chapter on report writing, we looked at storyboarding as a technique for integrating text and graphics (pages 144–145). We strongly recommend you adopt this approach so that text and graphic can be complementary to each other and not as bolt on extras.

Remember that your audience may not find the graphics as easy to understand as you do. This may be for some of these reasons.

A number of people just do not want to see any graphics. They build up a mental wall against tables or graphs *'I'll never understand this approach'*, they say, *'It's too mathematical and looks just too difficult'*.

For most of the time you will be communicating with people who have had some kind of scientific or technical education. But there will be times when you will wish to communicate to a wider audience so you might wish to minimize the technical and mathematical aspects.

- Do make sure that the pathways are clear, the sequence is obvious – which 'bits' relate to which.
- Pay particular attention to x and y axes in the graphs and the way that certain assumptions to do with scale are made explicit.

Activity

What are some of the advantages and disadvantages of using graphics to communicate? Before reading our list jot down your own response.

Graphics used appropriately and in a complementary way to text can:

- simplify very complex events, e.g. power surges
- show trends more easily than words – rises/falls in productivity
- dramatize particulate effects – sudden shifts
- complement the written work – so that we have a written explanation of failures in an operating system which is then followed by a graph highlighting these.

The *disadvantages*

- graphics may distort the picture. For instance, just showing the last few years' trend on our graphic can distort the real picture

- graphics may actually lie because of the way the scale has been manipulated
- graphics will not make poorly written ambiguous text easier to read
- graphics may overwhelm the written word.

Some principles in the use of graphics

We cannot lay down any precise rules for the use of graphics, much will depend on the house style of the organization you are working in. Here is some guidance for you:

- Graphics need to be planned for in any written or spoken 'text' rather than simply plonked in – hence the virtues of storyboarding.
- Graphics will not rescue poorly written texts or spoken presentations.
- It is vital to quote the sources of your material and the date. Your credibility may well be determined by the acceptability of the sources you quote. Do be careful over copyright. You will need to clear this if you are copying material and using it for public show.
- Think carefully of the nature of the scale of the graphics. You don't want to overwhelm the text or the spoken presentation with your graphics.
- Be bold. If you are using colour then avoid purples, light blues and yellows. It is highly likely, even with the cost of colour copying becoming more reasonable, that any copy will be in black and white and if you use these faint colours then much of your handiwork will disappear. Be bold in lettering and design.

Now here are some examples of the uses of graphics. We cannot in this short section do more than highlight the most commonly used ones. We supply reading material at the end which will provide you with more detail and a variety of applications.

The pie chart

This is an increasingly popular form of graphics. This is due to the fact that with the increasing use of computer packages such as Excel it is so much easier to construct and paste these into your document. This very ease has led to a rash of pie charts – Pie Chartitis we could call it. These charts are excellent for depicting bold clear distinctions and differences, for example, suppose we wanted to depict how first year students in engineering broke down into the main disciplines, we could devise a pie chart such as in Figure 18.1 on the next page.

When you plan your pie chart you will need to consider carefully how it will appear to your viewer or reader. We need to clearly label the various segments and make certain that the percentages are identified. It is worth

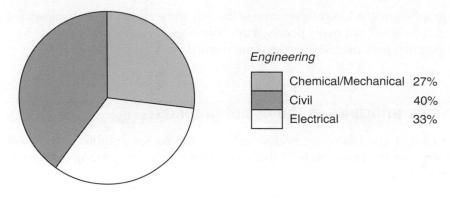

Figure 18.1

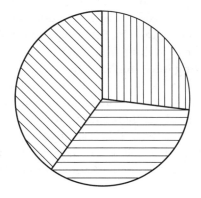

Figure 18.2

experimenting with various shadings and stippling effects so that the resulting chart is clear and doesn't cause swimming effects in front of the eyes. The pie chart in Figure 18.2 for instance might have that alarming effect.

Suppose however, that we wanted to depict how our first-year engineering students were broken down in terms of mature students, those coming straight from school, those coming from overseas, exchange students from the European Union (EU) and those coming after one or more years work experience but under 25 years of age. The divisions are rather lopsided, with one large segment, several small ones and one which represents a mere 1%, as shown in Figure 18.3.

This is not nearly so satisfactory for the reader. With the development of computer packages it is now possible to float one segment out of the chart and highlight it for attention. In Figure 18.4 we see the numbers representing overseas students entering the department (non-EU) as a separate segment. However, because we are faced with some very small slices it would be better to consider another form of graphical representation.

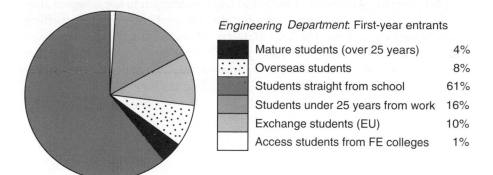

Engineering Department: First-year entrants

■	Mature students (over 25 years)	4%
	Overseas students	8%
	Students straight from school	61%
	Students under 25 years from work	16%
	Exchange students (EU)	10%
	Access students from FE colleges	1%

Figure 18.3

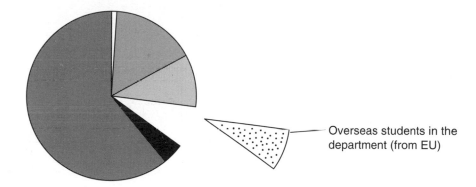

Overseas students in the
department (from EU)

Figure 18.4

Histograms

Again these are becoming increasingly popular. We see them used a great deal on TV news and documentary programmes. They have an immediate visual appeal. They are useful for showing the general distribution of data.

This is very useful in showing relationships. Let us examine those first-year engineering students. Let us suppose we wanted to analyse their end of year exam results. The raw data for their mathematics results shows us this:

Percentages	Number of students
70–90	1
60–70	5
50–60	20
40–50	15
30–40	10
10–30	5

This is interesting but we might want to use a histogram to see whether there are any patterns that emerge from the data, any particular bunching effects. In the histogram in Figure 18.5 the pattern of results stands out more clearly than in the simple listing. It is obvious that marks in mathematics were bunched in the 49–59 range while comparatively few came in the extremes of under 30 (thank goodness) or above 70 (a few geniuses!).

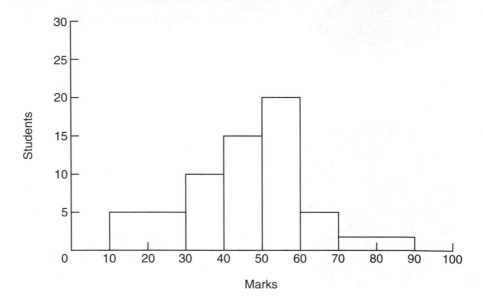

Figure 18.5

Bar charts

These provide a fairly simple way of showing data. They can have a number of different appearances depending on which bit of data you wish to stack on which. For instance, thinking of our first-year students again we might wish to depict the balance of their course over various years in terms of amount of time spent on various key disciplines. We could do this by the use of stacking the different topics on one another and reading off the proportions. The chart in Figure 18.6 shows how first years have a comparatively light timetable compared with the third years.

These charts can be very successful in depicting broad patterns. You will need to supply a key for the reader as to what the various patterns and shadings represent. These charts show the broad picture. It is a good idea in bar charts to separate out various stipple effects with white or dark so that they don't cause a swimming effect on your readers, see Figure 18.7.

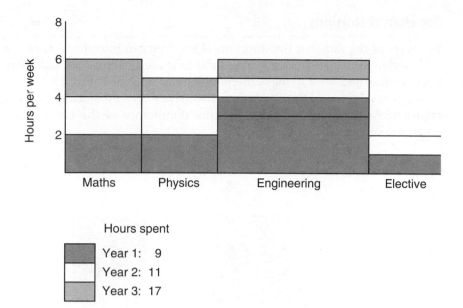

Figure 18.6

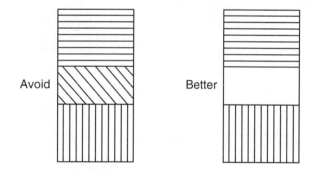

Figure 18.7

Bar chart distortions

Be aware of the fact that the direction of shading can introduce an element of distortion or bias – vertical stripes tend to make the bars look taller while horizontal stripes tend to make them look broader, as in Figure 18.8.

The actual layout of the charts may also have a small distorting effect, see Figure 18.9. In this sideways version the dominance of the longest bar is given prominence.

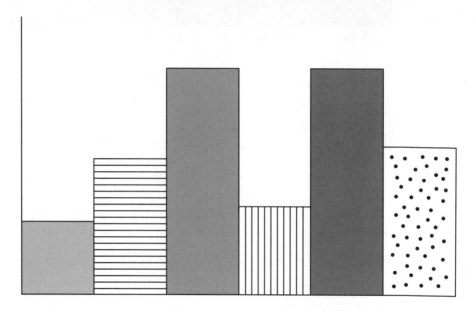

Figure 18.8

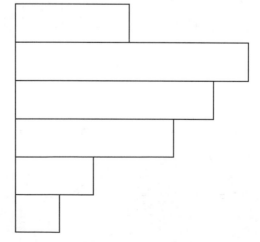

Figure 18.9

Whereas in Figure 18.10 the prominence of the tallest bar is less obvious.

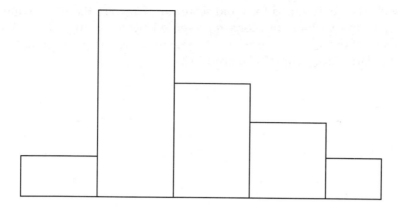

Figure 18.10

Gantt charts

This is a kind of flow chart in which one can see at a glance a programme of activities – the planned starting and finishing point. For instance our hard-working group of engineering students might well have to complete a number of lab reports in their first year. We could show this through a Gantt chart, see Figure 18.11.

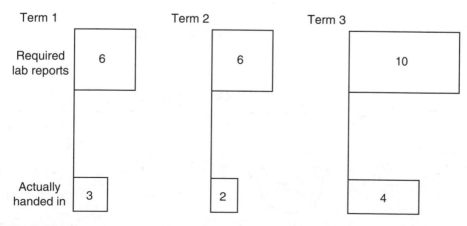

Figure 18.11

Flow charts

Flow charts are designed for rapid scanning. They are there to save words, they join the various decisions represented by lines; the charts depict a sequence of processes or decisions. There are clearly defined symbols which are standard. An example is Figure 18.12.

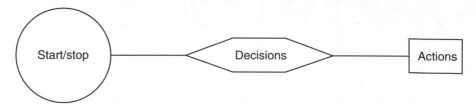

Figure 18.12

We could provide such a flow chart to assist our by now very hard-working first-year engineering students to find their way (hopefully!) through a laboratory sequence, see Figure 18.13.

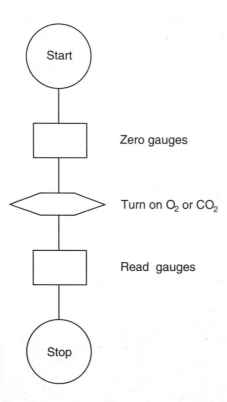

Figure 18.13

Diagrams

The aim here is to represent actions in a similar way to a flow chart but without the necessary symbols. The key word here is simplification. A diagram is a representation of something, rather as a cartoon is a simplification – the key features of the person – the nose, a twist of hair, the jut of a chin immediately reveal that well-known person. The same is true for a diagram. Diagrams are a kind of shorthand. As with any shorthand you need to be able to translate it. Shorthand is fine if you know that your reader or audience can perform this translation. When you draw a diagram you must remember those key principles we listed earlier. Because diagrams are shorthand then words are often needed to complement them. Our first years may well have been confronted by the diagram shown in Figure 18.14.

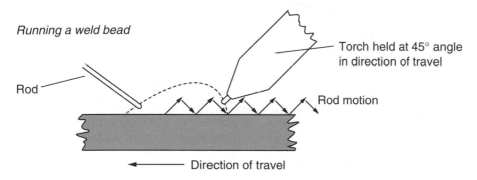

Running a weld bead

Torch held at 45° angle in direction of travel

Rod

Rod motion

Direction of travel

Figure 18.14

x, y Graphs

Most of you reading this will be very familiar with the typical x, y co-ordinates which are used to analyse the relationship between two parameters.

The very fact that we are so familiar with graphs like this should give us cause to stop and think a little. We should put ourselves in the position of our reader/viewer and ask some simple questions:

- What type of relationship are we in fact plotting?
- Should all the points be included? If not why not?
- Why have we adopted the scale that we have (i.e. would a different scale improve the communication of the data?).
- Are we missing out on any other information which could inform the graph – other tests?
- Have we supplied enough background information or commentary to enable our reader/viewer to gain the most from this graph?

The effect of scale

You are probably aware of this but here's a demonstration to emphasize this point. Compare the graph in Figure 18.15

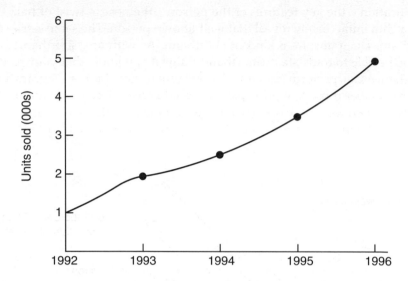

Figure 18.15

with the graph in Figure 18.16

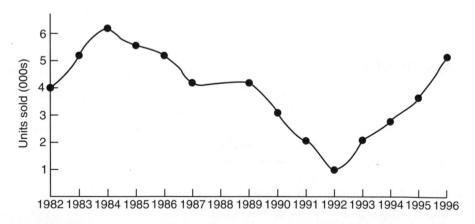

Figure 18.16

This second one is much more sensational than the first – so think very carefully about which scale you make use of.

How much information can you place on the one graph?

It is interesting to plot several variables on the one graph but you must consider the potential overload factor. Again, if we assume that we are not using bold colour then we have to consider carefully what will be the most effective way of differentiating between the variables.

We can use different types of line:

dotted	· ·
straight line	————————————————————
straight bold	————————————————————
chained	——— × ——— × ——— × ——— ×

Example: do you find the graph in Figure 18.17 reasonable in terms of the number of variables plotted?

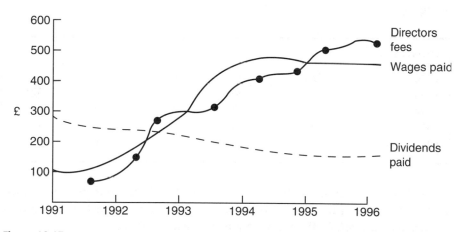

Figure 18.17

Tables

We have been used to seeing tables for a long time, certainly before the days of computers. They are always worth thinking about. The point we made earlier about experimenting with the layout of the information in your graphic is particularly important when it comes to designing tables. Generally avoid long thin tables. You've probably had the experience of reading a table and your eyes jumping from one column to the next. This is bound to happen as horizontal lines of figures march away left to right. Think instead of shorter, stubbier tables.

Let's go back to our first-year students. Suppose we need to know how many students have been taken on for engineering in the four universities within our region over the last five years, then we could construct the table like this:

Table (a)

		YEAR				
		1992	1993	1994	1995	1996
University	A	203	205	211	215	226
	B	175	189	187	196	198
	C	296	312	326	345	367
	D	196	198	179	187	202
	E	211	267	289	321	353

Or like this.

Table (b)

University	A	B	C	D	E
1996	226	198	367	202	353
1995	215	196	345	187	321
1994	211	187	326	179	289
1993	205	189	312	198	267
1992	203	175	296	196	211

Does this work out any better? Much will depend on what the aims of the table are. If you wish to direct your reader's attention to a particular trend by a particular university then table b will be easier to read.

Do experiment then with the layout of your tables.

Words can affect the visuals

We have said that words and graphics should be complementary – that is they both work together to produce understanding in the reader's mind. However, it is not generally recognized that the language we use can have a very large influence on the effect of our visual representation. They can affect the way the figures are interpreted.

Let us suppose that out of our hard-working first-year students, whose progress we have been following in this section, the numbers passing has *risen* by 8%. We could use:

- *climbed* by 8%

- *increased* by 8%
- *shot up* by 8%
- *crept up* by 8%
- *inched up* by 8%.

It is not difficult to separate out these words. Some are highly charged and emotive – *'shot up'*, *'inched'* as against the more neutral *'increased'*.

As engineers we must always be careful not to contaminate our visual representation by inappropriate or vague language.

We saw in the section on interviewing (page 43) that words like *'most'*; *'a few'*; *'some'*, and so on, are not only vague but can be very misleading when reporting results. Most can cover everything from 51 to 99%. We should make sure that our visuals do make clear what most actually is.

Here are some other tricky and slippery words which we must make sure that we anchor.

- *nearly* – is that 6.5 out of 10 or 8.5 out of 10?
- *minority* – i.e. 49.9%
- *majority* – 51.001%

We must be very careful with such common terms as *'average'*, *'normal'* and define what we mean. Always define what kind of average we are referring to. Are we for instance referring to the mean or the mode? Do watch out for the word *'relative'* and *'relatively'*. Very often such a term is used to make bad or uncomfortable news appear to be less so.

> *'Relatively few students failed the mathematics exam'.*

This might be phrased so as to reassure new entrants to the course that they don't have too much to worry about but the discerning reader may think rather differently!

Using graphics in oral presentations

Much of what we've said already applies to using graphics when talking to a group. However, there are some special considerations.

- Your audience does not have the advantage shared by your reader of being able to gaze up and down the table or bar chart and slowly absorb the information. If you make use of an overhead projector (OHP) or 35 mm slide the audience see the graphic and then it goes (and they're often left in the dark!).
- Graphics for an oral presentation therefore will need to be rethought – very few tables, charts, etc. taken from the printed page will be acceptable – they will need to be redrawn and often simplified. How often have you,

as part of an audience, had to sit through OHP slides which had been directly taken from a textbook and had to screw up your eyes to decipher the figures.

Here's an example of a visual taken from a written report. It shows completion rates from a certain university's engineering faculty over an 8-year period expressed as a percentage from the total intake.

	1986	1987	1988	1989	1990	1991	1992	1993	1994
Total	121	124	136	152	162	154	149	157	149
% fail	14	11	9	12	14	7	16	13	9

This we suggest would have to be re-cast in order for it to be more successful as a visual for an presentation.

Year	1992	1993	1994
Total students	149	157	149
% failures	16	13	9

Notice what has happened. The information to be visually displayed has been selected down: rather than a mass of figures right across the screen, we now have a concentration of key ones.

- Don't overload your listeners. Again they do not have the opportunity to browse. They can only absorb so much information at one sitting. Keep your visuals simple, bold and clear.
- Say to the audience if you are going to supply them with a papercopy of the visual. There's no point in telling them this after you've finished – by that time they may have started to scribble down as much as they can off the screen. They won't be very pleased with you for not telling them earlier, and secondly for giving them so much to do while they were supposed to be listening and absorbing the information.
- Think carefully of how you are going to slot your graphics into the presentation. It's a good idea to say and then show. In other words introduce and prepare your listeners for what they are going to see rather than spring surprises on them. Don't hurry the slide away, point out the relevant features. Take care how you do this. It's all too easy to mask the screen, flip chart or white board with your body.

In general depending on the size of the audience and the layout of the room it is best to adopt the position shown in Figure 18.18 when giving a presentation and referring to visuals.

Figure 18.18

Rather than the position shown in Figure 18.19.

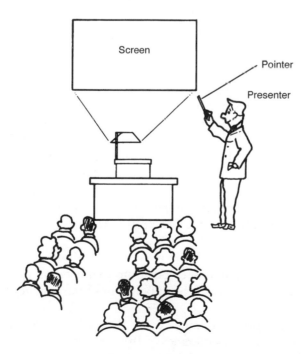

Figure 18.19

You might like to practise with a pointer (but please don't let it wave about in your hands – you're not conducting an audience or fencing with members of the front row!).

• With OHPs don't put too much on one slide. As a rule of thumb think of 6 × 6, that is:

No more than 6 words per line

No more than 6 lines per slide

Bullet points, not densely written texts

Plenty of space between the lines

Wide margins and plenty of headroom

Print in large font **(14 point bold)** and not in 12 point ordinary. Use a typeface which is clear – i.e. do not experiment with odd forms. You should consider not using a *serif* typeface, that is one which makes use of short finishing strokes or serifs, at the top and bottom of a letter. Typefaces which do not carry these are called *san serif* types. Helvetica – used in the above box – for instance is a san serif face.

• Striptease! Yes, how much do you reveal of your visual as you speak. Do you like presenters who take up a piece of paper and slowly drag this down in order to reveal the various points? (If you are bored with the talk you are probably waiting for that moment when the paper slips off the end and the careful striptease is brought to a rather hurried close!) You might like to adopt this procedure: firstly introduce the slide and set it for the audience:

'I'd now like to show you some figures relating to failure rates in the first year. These are taken from ... I have copies which I shall give out after ...'

Show the whole slide. Then cover or highlight with a light pen or washable OHP pen (different colour from that used on the screen) or point with a pointer – not a bit of broken pencil or shaking finger!).

• Do switch off, cover up, move away the visual when you have finished with it. So many presenters leave the OHP running and have to speak against the white noise and distraction for the audience of the white light.

- Do be sure to reposition or erase the visuals used by a previous speaker; they can very easily distract you and the audience, especially if they are interesting!

Summary

- Always think very carefully why you are using this graphic, make sure that it adds information and doesn't simply distract the reader or viewer.
- Don't overwhelm your reader or overload your listener with your graphics. A few, well chosen, can be much more effective than a whole series.
- Plan the way the graphics are slotted into the text or talk. Storyboarding can be very helpful for this.
- Try experimenting with pencil and paper before you rush to the computer.
- Make your graphics clear and bold in lettering, shape and design.
- Take the greatest care to quote the sources of any data and remember that scale can have a marked effect on the way your graphic can be interpreted.

Further reading

J W Davies (1995) *Communication for Engineering Students*. Longmans.
C Turk and J Kirkman (1989) *Effective Communication: Improving Scientific, Technical and Business Communication*, 2nd edition. E & F N Spon.

Part V

Part V

19

Communication and new technology

In this chapter we review some of the trends in the development of electronic communication; we revisit the concepts of redundancy and entropy together with Laswell's model. We provide hints for you when planning training in the new technology and conclude with practical hints for buying computer equipment on a budget.

This chapter is particularly difficult to write. The pace of technological change in electronic communication is hectic. What is novel today may well become old hat within 18 months or less. Take the case of the Internet. A couple of years ago this was limited to academic institutions, research-based firms, etc. Now it is possible to walk down many high streets, have a coffee at the Internet cafe, buy into the World Wide Web (WWW), go to your local computer store and for a modest sum purchase the necessary links for the most humble PC to be part of a world-wide communication system.

A similar example of rapid change can be seen in teleconferencing. Only a few years ago this facility was limited to major international companies that had constructed teleconferencing studios in their basements where senior executives could hold meetings, via large TV screens, with colleagues in the US, Australia, etc. Many smaller organizations have installed teleconferencing facilities. The talk in the industry is that such facilities will in a few years' time be as common as the fax transmissions. Increasingly people will have video-phone links on their desks and the idea of video phoning will be as accepted now as ordinary voice-only phones.

Perhaps it is possible to talk about a sequence that many of these new developments share. First, the pioneer stage: this is when the first products are made; these are usually expensive, cumbersome and often limited in their appeal. Not so long ago portable video cameras were bulky and troublesome, now they can be small enough to fit into a handbag and are very reliable and easy to operate.

The second stage is one of consolidation and development: this is where the products are reduced in price, increased in sophistication and made ready for the third stage, the take-off. This is where teleconferencing is reaching, where mobile phones were recently and where faxing was a decade ago. These systems cease to become novelties and become ordinary and accepted.

Finally, there is the stage where the original concept is made to branch into all kinds of sophisticated byproducts and developments. Hence the original laptop computer has now become part of the modern mobile office with fax and Internet connections. Mobile telephones can now link to small-scale printers and fax machines to provide the user with truly global communications net.

As engineers, much of your time will be spent making use of the new technology. The mobile phone has made and is still making a vast difference to engineers on-site in terms of their ability to keep in touch with fast moving events. The electronic notepad enables an engineer to write notes (once the system has recognized the handwriting), then when he or she comes back to the site office these can be read by laser reader and converted into print as memos, reports, and so on. The advantages of such a system are enormous, especially when notes have to be written in hostile environments. Increasingly voice-in systems will replace the keyboard. You talk and the text appears on the screen. Just remember, don't have a bad cold the day you compose that vital CV!

Effectiveness and efficiency in electronic communication

A great deal of research time is now being spent examining any differences that these developments are making to the communication processes. Certainly information is being passed more rapidly and efficiently. We must again differentiate between effectiveness and efficiency in communication as we have done several times in this book. More communication sent along the wires or cables might be considered efficient in terms of information passed through but that does not make it certain that the communication is effective. In other words the fax messages and information from laptops linked to mobile phones may pour in but that doesn't necessarily mean that these messages will be attended to. In fact the sheer deluge of electronic communication in many offices – e-mail, Internet, faxes, and increasingly video links, are in themselves causing problems. Staff increasingly ask:

- 'Which of these messages should I attend to first?'
- 'Which of these is really geared to my work?'
- 'Which of these can I trust?'

There is growing evidence that we are swamping colleagues and clients with what has been described as 'electronic bumph'. It appears from the evidence that it is increasingly easy to ignore an e-mail. Most of these electronic messages are composed quickly, frequently badly spelt and punctuated and they may, because of their speed of composition, actually miss the point completely. Engineers who would take time to draft a letter – carefully checked for errors – will be happy to shoot off an e-mail. In so doing they may ignore the need for appropriate tone and sensitivity to their 'customer'. The result of all this could be *'worse'* communication from all these messages, not better.

We have to develop *'a need-to-know'* policy: i.e. to classify our 'audience' as:

* those who must have the information
* those who would find it of interest but not as a priority
* those who can be told where the information is so that they access it when they need to.

The integrity of communication

Electronic communication systems are also becoming more threatened with corruption through viruses, misuse, etc. It is fairly easy to see if your mail has been tampered with – the tearing of the envelope, suspicious retaping of seals, etc. – but much more difficult to discover if someone has entered your e-mail register, tapped into your mobile phone links, or put a nasty sleeping virus into the heart of your computer. The last decade has seen many of the devices that were previously associated with James Bond becoming part and parcel of commercial life: anti-bugging systems, equipment to electronic sweep a conference room before a vital meeting takes place, scanners to detect the presence of unwanted eavesdropping within the office as well as the shredder to make sure that those sensitive documents relating to contracts do not find their way to competitors.

Electronic communication and audits

The author has carried out a number of communication audits in public and private sectors. Very often staff in these institutions wish better communications with their bosses and bosses want better, swifter communication with their staff. But we have to ask what we mean by better communications? The ability that we now have to send instant communication creates opportunities as well as threats. In one organization being audited e-mail had been introduced so as to allow increased communication between departments. What was happening after the system had been installed for a year was that the airwaves of e-mail were being filled with small talk, social events, mixed in with memos, notices of meetings, announcements from various sports clubs and staff committees, etc. Some kind of route ways had to be organized, so that an important communication did not get lost in the middle of other less vital ones. Most organizations now have a policy towards the use of internal communication systems to prevent this kind of problem. However, having a policy is one thing; making sure that it actually works is quite another!

Effective electronic communication can be analysed in terms of the Laswell model that we examined at the start of this book, page 8.

- *Who?*
- *Says what?*
- *In which channel?*
- *To whom? When?*
- *With what effect?*

The very fact that we can so easily communicate nowadays means that we may have to think that little bit more about *why* and *when* and *for whom* we press that button, dial that number, send that fax on its way, or plug into the Internet with a message.

Entropy and redundancy

Communications theory, as we saw in Chapter 1, makes use of two concepts which might be useful to us when dealing with the ease of communication as represented by the new electronic communication: redundancy and entropy.

Redundancy as we saw is that kind of communication which is normal, expeced, predictable, stable, familiar, etc. The very ease of sending communications electronically may mean that our communications can become more redundant – less noticed than before. If all messages are routinely faxed then where is the priority that used to be reserved for that special faxed message – the others all came though the post. If an international phone call was only used for special news – urgent and personal, then all those words pouring along the Internet probably will not carry that same sense of urgency; because of this such a message may be disregarded.

Perhaps another example of this difference between the two forms would help. Suppose a member of staff is ill and has had to take sick leave. Her boss knows that she is on the e-mail link. Many staff have this facility at home which is useful when they don't have to come into the office, when they are busy on another site or when because of adverse weather conditions, strikes on the rail network, etc., it's difficult, if not impossible to get to work. So her boss, knowing that she has this facility sends her an e-mail in which he hopes that she makes a speedy recovery. This, given the steady stream of e-mails that will be pouring in from her office, goes by fairly unnoticed – it doesn't make much of a stir. However, if the same boss had sent her a hand-written note posted to her home written in ink on real note paper and personally signed (as opposed to a sheet of photocopying paper with a secretary's signature), then this would be highly entropic, more likely to be noticed and it might well have more impact than that e-mail.

All this is not to say that modern technology of communications has not got a great deal of very real advantages. We must however be careful not to confuse more communication – the sheer volume of messages – with effectiveness of those messages.

Training for the technology

Keeping in mind these points we now turn to you, an engineer, making use of this technology. There are several ways in which you as a newcomer to a system can become proficient in its use. Firstly, there are the manuals. Some of these are large and bulky, others are slim and highly readable. The fact is that most people do not read them. Perhaps they do not willingly connect the old (paper) communication with the new (electronic) variety.

Secondly, you could go for coaching; this can range from sitting next to 'Nellie' – i.e. someone who has used the system before and perhaps is one step ahead, to someone who really is expert on the system and can provide you with on-going support. Alternatively you could attend training courses. How to use X program on your computer – three half-day sessions will guarantee that you can double your existing ability to write crisp reports and clear all those letters from your in-tray!

The evidence is that many people muddle their way through all these various options. We would recommend that you consider a plan and that you tap into all these options. Firstly, remember that most electronic systems of communication are fairly robust. Very few people have 'broken' a computer by hitting a few 'wrong' keys. Once you've found out how to switch the thing on and off then we suggest that you experiment with it under supervision. Then read the manual. But don't try and remember everything or do all the exercises. Ask advice from colleagues about which operations of the system are crucial for you to know about. So many people start trying to learn quite intricate approaches which they will hardly ever use. Ask any experienced user of a system about just how many operations he or she uses and you they might well answer 20%. If you consider the power of modern computer packages, think of the one you use most, then it would be unusual for you to be making more than 50% use of its many applications. So keep it simple. Don't bother trying to master the extras before you've got the basics. Going on training courses can be very useful but you must ask yourself some questions before you sign up:

- Will this course feature the systems, the equipment that I will in fact be using? (It's obviously going to be more difficult if you have to apply what you've been told and shown to another type of system with different formats and controls.)
- Will the training feature the kind of exercises and applications that you will be needing to use in your work? It's often fun to be working on someone else's case material but again you will have the problem of having to translate that into your applications.
- Will the trainer appreciate my particular concerns – is he or she sufficiently tuned into my needs? This is often a problem if you work in a very small organization when the training is geared to the requirements of those with fewer staff resources and much more limited equipment.

There will be other questions relating to cost and convenience but these are probably a great deal less important that the ones we've outlined above. It might be more effective to pay a little more and suffer rather more inconvenience to join a course which serves your particular needs than one that misses the mark. Do remember to ask about follow-up. So much will be forgotten after an intensive course. It is good to be able to phone up your tutor when you are actually experimenting with what you were told on the course.

Buying your equipment

There is so much on the market at the moment in terms of PC, printers, CD-ROM capability, connections to the Internet, etc., the trouble for students just starting off is that it all comes rather dear. Having said that the real cost of much of this equipment is coming down. The author spent over £3000 five years ago on PC software and laser printer; that same package (considerably enhanced in capability) would now cost under £1500.

Hard-up students who are increasingly required to word process their essays, dissertations, lab reports have the following options:

- Pay someone to do this work – expensive except for a final dissertation or CV – and you lose control.
- Use only the computer facilities within your university – fine but it is good to have the ability to work away in your flat or hall of residence.
- Buy second-hand machines – always an option but you have to face it that they are likely to crash. You might consider equipment from previous generations – many writers are still using Amstrads with a format that is completely non-standard.

Basically you have to decide what it is that you *have to do* rather than what the computer stores invite you to dream about. For instance, you may only need a basic word processing with text-editing facility. It's nice to have elaborate software programs available to paste in all those superb graphics but don't forget that just by leaving a space in your text and using some simple geometrical instruments you can create most of these charts, histograms and graphs.

You don't have to buy a printer. As long as you can pound out the text in your flat, hall of residence you can always take it up to be printed at the university/college.

You don't have to buy a monitor. Some older models will allow you to plug into a TV set. It is quite possible to scour the pages of your local newspaper to find such models for under £100. This is not a big investment even if you only get 18 months use.

The other option is to buy the most basic laptop computer you can find by shopping around. If you go for a black and white screen you will find that prices are much lower than for colour and there is now a reasonable second-hand market in these. Look at university notice boards and notices in shop windows. Coloured screens are certainly easier on the eye and more pleasant to work on, but these trimmings can wait until you're a well-paid engineer!

Summary

- Engineers are finding the new mobile and lightweight forms of communication of real assistance in their work, especially on-site.
- We must be careful not to confuse effectiveness with efficiency in our use of the new electronic communication – e-mail being a case in point. Older forms of communication may be more effective in certain situations.
- It is worth thinking carefully about what kind of training in the new communications technology is most effective for you. A follow-up to training is often essential.
- There are computer systems available for those with small budgets.

Further reading

Current computer magazines.
IT departments of your university/organization.
The IT section of newspapers such as *The Times, The Telegraph, The Independent, The Guardian, The Scotsman, The Herald* and their Sunday equivalents.
IT sections of *The Economist* and *Newsweek*.

20

Conclusion

Here we are at the end of this particular journey. What can we now say are some of the key guiding principles of communication for engineers.

The subtitle of this book is *Bridge That Gap*. It is true that we often see communication as a gap – something to be avoided, but a gap can be seen as a pathway leading somewhere, a gap in the forest – an opportunity to move to somewhere better.

We have in this text concentrated on the failures in communication. Publicity tends to feature such failures by engineers, their lapses and the disasters or complications that allow such lapses. We have quoted a few of these in this book. However, we should also see in so many completed and successful engineering projects evidence that none of these projects could have succeeded in being completed on time without clear and effective communication from engineer to engineer and from engineers to all those others engaged on the work. This is true whether the project is civil – the motorway or bridge completed ahead of schedule, chemical – the development of a new refining process; electrical – the new ignition system in the new model, or mechanical – an improved oil extraction process for the North Sea. Running all the way through successful projects is the theme of good communication: the patient and detailed negotiation, the careful listening, the checking and securing of understanding. We should celebrate these and make sure that engineers take pride in such achievements.

As part of such a celebration and as a pointer to the future we hope that this book has been of use and will continue to be of use whether you are just starting your life as an engineer or whether you are firmly established on that road. Here are then some key principles to leave you with.

- *Before you communicate consider your audience*
  This is a theme we have constantly 'hammered home' throughout this text. A communication is a two-way process. We can give the most splendid presentation and write the most crisp and persuasive report but if no one listens and no one is persuaded then what have we communicated?

  Before you communicate ask questions, try and find out what your audience/readership is likely to consist of. Try and establish what their expectations are so that you reduce the risk of disappointing them. This is basic customer care. Your audience is your customer. Care for them so that real communication can take place and that a good business relationship can be established.

- *No one is a born communicator.*
  Much of the competence and success in communication comes about from observation of others, seeing how they manage, assessing their strengths and weakness and learning from these. We can never just copy what others do but we can by observation learn techniques and procedures, methods and approaches that we can adapt to our own needs.

  After reading this book there's no need to be bored during those idle moments at meetings (yours will be much better now that you've read and absorbed the lesson in Chapter 9) or at airports, stations, conferences, etc. You will be able to observe your fellow communicators and learn something from what they do or fail to do. Ask yourselves why is this person now being successful in this communication? Why is he or she gaining the audience's attention (or rapidly losing it?). Why does this person's reports always seem to get referred to and actually read when the ones I labour over just lie about the office unnoticed, gathering dust.

- *Communication must be seen in its context.*
  We are seldom if ever communicating in a vacuum. We have used the term appropriate a good deal. The good communicator is not just someone who has a range of techniques but is also sensitive and aware of the appropriacy of what he or she is writing or speaking about. He or she is also sensitive to the leakage, the feedback coming from others, the subtle and not so subtle comments from your audience. Sensitive communicators are 'cue conscious'; they take note of this and avoid blundering on. They can read the warning signs.

- *An increasingly important part of this appropriateness comes with a awareness of cultural dimension.*
  We haven't had much opportunity to go into depth on this topic, but increasingly engineers are operating in multicultural dimensions, for instance building that refinery in Cambodia. This will require more than just competent technical communication; it needs a sensitivity and awareness of the cultural dimensions – the barriers and pitfalls that abound when someone is communicating outside their own culture. (Do you shake hands when a Cambodian engineer is bowing to you?)

- *The interdependence of the various forms of communication.*
  Although we have divided this text into a number of separate sections we have tried to integrate a variety of aspects so that they are not seen in watertight compartments. (Remember the *Titanic* sank even with watertight compartments!)

  It is obvious that you need to be as competent a listener as you do to be a speaker, to be a successful interviewer. (God has give us two ears and one mouth so that's the right proportion of time between speaking and listening!) It's obvious too that in order to be competent on the telephone you need to be able to listen carefully and adopt a non-threatening or bored tone of voice. That these things are so obvious we feel is still a good reason for emphasizing them here. It's often the obvious points that get forgotten or ignored.

- *Communication as personal development.*
  This may come about as a result of an appraisal or feedback from a manager

or client. We've already said that you can learn a great deal from observation of others. Secondly, you can do some of the follow-up reading we have listed at the end of each section of this text. Thirdly, you can attend a course in one of the areas where you feel your skills need to be improved.

There are now a bewildering number of communication skills courses on offer – everything from specialized training costing hundreds of pounds per day to evening classes, Open University courses, etc., which will only set you back a few pounds per session. If you are a very busy person and find it difficult to attend such courses or because your needs are very specialized then you might want to consider coaching. This is where you find someone to coach you in a specific skill such as interviewing or presentation. Your coach needs to be someone who is competent and experienced (not always the same thing!) in the desired area of skills enhancement, and who will, like a sports coach, be prepared to sit with you and give you encouragement and feedback on performance together with tips as to how to advance in that particular skill.

Communication is a skill and like all skills it needs to be rehearsed and rehearsed. If you drive a car then you will not be aware of how you change gear, but remember those first weeks and months when you had to concentrate so much on changing gear; those times when you forgot to change up and those embarrassing moments at busy junctions when you stalled. Now all this has become a smooth operation; it just happens. Well, this smooth delivery occurs when you have practised a communication skill until such time that it becomes natural and almost subconscious. For instance, if you haven't made many presentations then you will consciously have to remember to sweep your eyes around the audience instead of settling on one friendly face. After you have done some 50 of these then you will be sweeping the audience without realizing that you are doing it. It has become natural.

A communication audit for yourself

Now that you've read the book it might be interesting and useful for you to run a communication skills audit on yourself. It could be something as simple as listing:

What do I think are my strengths?	Where do I feel I need to build?

Many people are reluctant to acknowledge their communication strengths – they think it's showing off and being immodest. Yet it is important to know your strengths; for one thing it will help you to contribute to group work.

Knowledge of your deficits means that you are half-way to being able to put matters right. As we stated at the beginning of this book, engineers have perhaps been too unwilling to carry out this kind of audit and improve their communication skills.

Don't neglect the opportunities provided by TV, film and video. There are so many programmes, documentaries in particular, which feature aspects of communication success and failure. For example: lessons from the Bophal chemical disaster. How the hole in the ozone layer was discovered. The latest laser detector for speeding motorists!

You can learn a great deal from these sources as well as from fiction – science fiction often proves to be a most interesting and apt source of insights into communication; think of the computer HAL in the book and film of 2001 Space Odyssey – the intelligent machine that refuses to obey orders from its human masters!

Well this completes this particular odyssey. Good luck with all your communications in bridging that gap!

21

Your tool box

There are some very important 'tools' that you will need to use when communicating. This 'box' is only modest in size and scope; we refer you to books which will enlarge this collection.

A use of language

Some practical hints on word processing

We've discussed the process of 'getting started' when writing. Some people find it best after they have drawn up an outline to get straight onto the word processor and fire away. Others like to put down a draft in pencil or pen and then transfer that into the word processor. Do remember that the organization where you work may well have a house style which you should keep to in terms of layout and style of writing.

Here are some tips:

- Find a word processing package that suits your needs as an engineer; for instance, one which has on it the mathematical, chemical, etc., signs and symbols that you will need in your work. Get to use it before you have to write any major document such as a thesis. As we said in Chapter 19, try and find someone who will give you some coaching. Reading the manual is one thing and it is useful but most people find a coach very valuable, someone with plenty of patience and who really knows the system, including the short cuts. Most people find that they learn a great deal more this way than simply by reading the manual. Be brave and try things out with your word processing package. As we said most modern systems are pretty robust and you won't break anything.
- Do remember to save your material as you go along.
- Do back up your material on another disk as well as the hard disk of the computer you are using. Too many important pieces of work have been lost by not taking this elementary precaution. Label your disks clearly and store them safely, i.e. not on that radiator!
- You will be able to select from a wide variety of type sizes and fonts (designs of the typeface). Experiment with different typefaces and fonts by all means but remember that there may be a 'house style' – that is the agreed way of setting out the text, use of typeface, etc.

This text is printed in Palatino. Most assessments of readability suggest that something between 11–13 type size is most readable. You will also have to decide whether you are going for right-hand justification – that is where the lines all end at the same margin on the right-hand margin as with this text. There is some evidence that this layout makes the text a little easier to read – that is why newspapers make use of columns. Try not to have lines of print which are too long. The best way to judge this is to see if you can easily read a whole block of your text; if your eyes are having to refocus too often and if you start jumping lines then not only are the lines probably too long but also too close together.

Try printing shorter lines and open up the space between them (again think of newspapers), long straggly lines do present problems for your readers.

- Remember that too much variety of typeface and font within a single text will only be confusing for your reader. Sudden shifts from Times 12 point to Helvetica 10 will only irritate. Likewise think carefully about the way you make use of **bold**, <u>underlining</u>, *italics* and CAPITALS – use these possibilities sparingly. Although printing the odd word in capitals makes it stand out whole lines of upper-case will reduce its readability. Likewise overuse of bold will diminish its impact. You might want to limit your use of italics to references and quotations. Think carefully about using underlining. If the text is well written you will not need to put in very much emphasis.

Spacing: basically one space after a comma; two after a colon, semi-colon or full stop. Be careful to keep this consistent and avoid this:

Do not leave any space, however, before a full stop.

You will notice that the above line has been *indented* under the previous ones. Again, indentation of paragraphs may well be part of the house style you are working with.

In many reports it is the normal practice not to indent but to leave blank spaces between paragraphs as above.

Checking your work: spelling

Basically don't rely on spell "chekkers"! They have a use in providing you with an overview but you will need to do some serious proof-reading in order to spot all possible errors. For instance this text:

To many people are two dependant on word processing programmes to cheque there texts.

passed through a spell checker will come out correct. This is because the various words are in its dictionary and it doesn't recognize the difference between homophones – that is words that sound the same but are different, as are to and too. The text should have read:

Too many people are **too** depend**ent** on word processing **programs** to **check their** texts.

Hints for proof-reading your text (or someone else's)

- Always use a different colour ink from the original.
- Mark clearly on the top of the line the alteration.
- Make double certain that your 'correction' is in fact correct!

If you did the exercise on pages 148–149 then this is how you should have proofed it.
The bold italic version is the correct one!

Millions Cant Spell Properely
Millions Can't Spell Properly

Acording to a survey by Gallup of 1000 adults only
According to a survey by Gallup of 1000 adults, only
one in six adults scored full markes in a test of
one in six adult scored full marks in a test of
six familliar words; necessery, accomodation,
six familiar words: necessary, accommodation,
sincerly ,business, separate and height.
sincerely, business, separate and height.
Height proved, the easiest word with 84 per cent
Height proved the easiest word with 84 per cent
spelling it correctly while only 27 percent were
spelling it correctly while only 27 per cent were
able to spell accommodation.
able to spell accommodation.
At least 40 per cent of the women survey got five
At least 40 per cent of the women surveyed got five
or more words right compared with just 30 per
or more words right compared with just 30 per
cent of men. Only 12 per cent of those aged 16- 25
cent of men. Only 12 per cent of those aged 16-25
got all 6 words corect while 21 percent of those
got all 6 words correct while 21 per cent of those
over 65 years did;It is dificult to judge wether
over 65 years did; it is difficult to judge whether
standards of spelling are improved or not
standards of spelling are improving or not.

Did you manage to spot all those errors? If you did well done. Now most of the spelling errors would be picked up by your spell checker, but there are a number of other errors, to do with inconsistencies (per cent or percent), punctuation (the final full stop) and grammar (are improved/improving).

Homophones you have loved (and lost!)

As we have noted, one of the problems with spell checkers is that they fail to recognize the difference between homophones – that is words which have the same sounds but are different in meanings. As an example we could note stationery and stationary. Apart from some quick ways of remembering the difference (e.g. e for envelopes in stationery), these differences have to be learnt. A dictionary should help you. Here are a few to remember:

affect (*verb*): colds affect him badly
effect (*noun*): the effect of a recent cold on his breathing

compliment (*noun*): that's a nice compliment on his work
(*verb*): I compliment you on that great effort
complement: this new style will complement the existing design

counsel (**verb**) I counsel you to think very carefully about this advice
(*noun*) I asked her counsel for advice
council (*noun*) The town council will require you to pay immediately

ensure (*verb*) This lock will ensure your safety
insure (*verb*) Do insure your new computer

its (*possessive pronoun*) The table's lost its balance
it's (*contraction for it is*) It's here on the table

passed (*verb*) He passed by the accident sign
past (*adjective*) Your past performance has not been good enough

personal (*adjective*) This is a personal memo
personnel (*noun*) Take this round all personnel before close of business

principle (*noun*) The principle of flight must be understood
principal (*noun*) The Principal of the college accepted the invitation
principal (*adjective*) His principal objection was that of cost.

practise (*verb*) He wanted to practise his keyboard skills
practice (*noun*) the practice of law

their (*possessive pronoun*) their book
there (*adverb*) The book is over there
they're (*contraction for they are*) They're in pretty poor condition.

Exercise

Underline the correct word in this list. Answers underneath

1. The financial difficulties affected/effected him badly.
2. Could you please test the current/currant on this wire.
3. His future is dependent/dependant on his passing these exams.
4. It was a triumph; an historic/historical ascent of Everest.
5. We license/licence you to drive this lorry.
6. She emigrated/immigrated into the UK.
7. She practises/practices law in the city.
8. The glass was in a stationery/stationary position.
9. The waste/waist left over after the event was enormous.
10. The referee must be disinterested/uninterested in the verdict.

Answers

1. The financial difficulties affected him badly.
2. Could you please test the current on this wire.
3. His future is dependent on his passing these exams.
4. It was a triumph; an historic ascent of Everest.
5. We license you to drive this lorry.
6. She immigrated into the UK.
7. She practises law in the city.
8. The glass was in a stationary position.
9. The waste left over after the event was enormous.
10. The referee must be disinterested in the verdict.

US English rules okay

Remember that many word processors have been installed with *Webster's* American dictionary. So when you are printing out your CV just check that you haven't put down driving license (US) when you really mean driving licence (British)!

Most people are aware of the obvious differences between US and British English. When you work overseas you need to recognize that many engineers who will be communicating with you have themselves been taught American English. You will need to be sensitive to the differences.

Exercise

How would you translate this extract written in US English into the British version.

Test Driver's Report

In performing the high speed test, I was traveling at 135 mph and had gotten the test auto under control but on the second corner it suddenly dove away from me and I ended up with a catalog of problems: the tires failed to grip, the windshield gave way, and the hood ended up dented. My suggestion is that we ax the program with Ford and cut any dialog with their Test Center even if their attorney sues us for our last cent.

Possible 'translation' into British English

Test Driver's Report

In performing the high speed test, I was **travelling** at 135 mph and had got the car under control but on the second corner it suddenly **dived** away from me; and I ended up with a **catalogue** of problems: the **tyres** failed to grip, the **windscreen** gave way and the **bonnet** ended up dented. My suggestion is that we axe the **programme** with Ford and discontinue dialogue with their Test **Centre** even if their **lawyer** sues us for our last **penny**.

Punctuation

The comma

There are over 18 uses of the comma. We cannot cover each one. Here though are some key uses:

After an although/however phrase before the main part of the sentence, for example

Although the nut had been checked, it did come loose

- Certain expressions such as however, moreover, thereafter when placed in the middle of the sentence, for example

Her greatest success, however, was in physics
- For emphasis. What is the difference between these two sentences:

Please apply in writing before the end of March
Please reply, in writing, before the end of March

The second sentence with in writing surrounded by commas implies an emphasis – i.e. please put it into writing, don't phone us or come and see us in the office.

Using commas is a much more subtle way of creating emphasis than say underlining or placing words in bold or capitals. These can have the effect of shouting at your reader.

The next use of the comma is rather more difficult. In essence it is all about the difference between that and which. Look at these two sentences and see if you can appreciate what the essential difference is:

The computers, which are on the table, are available for sale

The computers that are on the table are available for sale

Here in the second sentence, *'that are on the table'* identifies the type of computer and is restrictive. There is an implication here that there are a number of computers but only those actually on the table will be available for sale. In the first one the phrase, *which are on the table* is not restrictive; this means that it can be left out without altering the sense of the sentence.

The semi-colon

This indicates a very close relationship between the parts of the sentence it separates. It is used where you want to break a sentence into two fairly equal parts, for example

Several safety systems use the procedures document; others have ignored it

It can also be used to separate out parts of a sentence where there is no connective word or phrase as in instructions:

Do not replace handset; re-dial number

The colon

This signifies to the reader that the part of the sentence following on adds to, elaborates or clarifies the preceding statement.

These were the conclusions: the engine was to be dismantled and the maintenance regime to be reviewed.

The dash

This is used to indicate a separate and unrelated thought arising from the sentence, for example

The lab reports have consistently pointed to the need for new techniques to be used – and just think of all the benefits for us.

Hyphens
Another tricky area. This is where a dictionary will be of real help, especially the fuller variety.

Exercise

Examine this list carefully, which word would you hyphenate and where?

cooperation   proofread   standalone   misspelled   impossible   redial   handset   telephone   Anglo American   self satisfaction   father in law   postwar   diskdrive   recover   online

---

You would be *unusual* if you used the hyphen in: tele-phone hand-set. These words are seldom if ever hyphenated.

You *could certainly* hyphenate:

> co-operation   re-dial   stand-alone
> proof-read   disk-drive
> mis-spelled   post-war

You might have felt that the repetition of the double *ss* in misspelling and the double *oo* in cooperation looked ugly and that it was conventional to use the hyphen with the others.

You *should have used* the hyphen in

> Anglo-American   father-in-law   self-satisfaction

Most dictionaries would say that this is a requirement.

You *would* use the hyphen for re-cover (your sofa) because you would have wanted to distinguish it from recover (from an illness).

Capitals
It is very important that you think through your use of capitals. There are certain definites:

- Beginning a sentence
- Proper names Mr Smith
- Titles: Dr, Prof., Mr, Head Teacher
- Headings, e.g. Findings, Conclusions.
- Copyright trade names, e.g. Kodak.
- Lists:
  Mount the frame
  Align the wires
- Acronyms when only the first letter of each word is used: UN (United Nations).

Avoid using capitals in blocks

THEY ARE REALLY QUITE DIFFICULT TO READ EN BLOCK WHEREAS SINGLE WORDS IN CAPS CAN BE EFFECTIVE IN DRAWING ATTENTION TO THEM, COMPARED WITH

NO SMOKING

The important thing is to be consistent in your use of capitals. Please avoid this kind of use:

Don't use Capitals when you are not Sure of What you want TO achieve such as this. THIS!

Sentences and paragraphs

The sentence is the basic building block of all our writing. A sentence is a unit of meaning that makes sense on its own. Some problems:

Length
Think of writing as you would digesting food. Too much at once produces indigestion. Consider as you write your sentences if you have said enough on that particular point.

Exercise

How would you chunk this sentence for easier reading?

The engineering students brainstormed a large range of potential uses for all the waste heat produced in in the furnace which ranged from heating water at a nearby fish farm to producing current of warm air to supply heat for workers at a local saw mill.

This is rather indigestible, i.e. when the reader has to stop because there is just too much in it. Here is a possible re-write:

The students of engineering brainstormed a large range of potential uses for the waste heat produced in the furnace. These ranged from heating water at a nearby fish farm to supplying heat for workers at a local saw mill.

Do be careful of writing nothing but short sentences, this can become very tiresome. Variety of sentence length makes your writing interesting to read. A shorter sentence placed in the middle of longer ones stands out; you therefore create emphasis.

Exercise

Have a close look at this 'beauty'. How would you improve its digestibility for the reader? Which sentence deserves to be emphasized?

This section has attempted to develop a fundamental concept of this new quality system as something totally novel in a civil aircraft, a concept which although it draws on some pervious work produced by the company has been greatly influenced by the specific needs of the client for a system which will provide many years' efficient working.

Possible re-write:

> This section has attempted to develop a fundamental concept for this new quality system. *It is something totally novel in a non-military aircraft.* It is a concept which draws on previous work by the company and is influenced by the needs of the client for a system which will provide many years' efficient working.

Notice how the key selling sentence (italicized) is given emphasis because it is shorter than the others.

Complexity

Long sentences are not the main problem; we can isolate the chunks and surround them with full stops. It is when the sentence is complex and confusing, then we have to do rather more radical surgery than just putting in a few full stops, for example

> A large range of potential uses which had emerged from the discussion and which looked promising although as yet only on paper were examined for their likely practicality.

Thus is not just a long sentence it is also complex. The backbone of a sentence is: *subject ... verb ... object*. In this sentence the subject: *'A large range of potential uses'* is separated from the verb *'were examined'* by two clauses, *'which had emerged from the discussion'* and *'which looked promising'*. Where this happens the reader has to 'hold' the subject in the memory until such time as he or she lands upon the verb and eventually the object, *'likely practicality'*.

Try to simplify the structure of your sentences. For instance bring the subject and the verb closer together, as in:

> A large range of potential uses were examined for their practicality. These were ones that had emerged from discussion and looked promising.

A famous writer on writing, Ambrose Bierce noted that:

Good writing is clear thinking made visible.

So do try and work out what it is you want to say; try and think it through so that the various steps are obvious and that your reader is able to see clearly your progress from one point to the next. Don't try and put too much into one sentence – it will break under the weight. Long sentences like long bridges need careful support!

Active or passive sentences

The difference here is essentially one of focus. Where do you wish the focus to be in this sentence.

> I placed the safety hatch firmly in position. (Active)

Here the focus is very much on me the person who did it. This might be appropriate if you wanted to single yourself out in terms of responsibility. I did it not anyone else. However, when we are reporting operations carried out as in lab reports and investigations we usually move ourselves away from centre stage and onto the sidelines. It is not 'we' who are important but what we actually did.

> The safety hatch was firmly placed in position. (Passive)

The passive, however, is often longer than the active.

> The electrical surge damaged the machine. (Active, six words)
> The machine was damaged by the surge in electricity. (Passive, nine words)

We saw on pages 155–156, in our chapter on lab reports that in using the passive, unnecessary lengthy phrasing often finds its way in. These include:

- *It is felt.*
- *It is thought.*
- *It is believed.*
- *It is hoped.*
- *It is suggested*, and so on.

Try and eliminate them from your writing; they are normally just adding.

The passive is useful where many individuals or departments were involved in a process or task and where you do not wish to personalize their contribution.

> John Smith, Senior Quality Controller, Allen Sharp, Chief Technician produced the system, Caroline Evans, Technical Author was responsible for documentation and Harry Peters, Head of Sales and Marketing successfully completed the negotiation.

It would be better to write:

> Our senior Quality Controller and Chief Technician produced the system, the Technical Author was responsible for all the documentation and the negotiations were successfully handled by the Head of Sales and Marketing.

Be very careful about using the passive when it comes to personal letters. The passive can sound very cold and impersonal. If a friend at university had failed her exams and had to leave the course how would she react to this kind of letter from administration.

> It is regretted that you have not succeeded in the June exams and that as a result you will not be able to enter the second year of the course. For further information please contact ...

Your friend would feel rather hurt by such a cold impersonal letter. It could be improved by putting it into the active.

> We are sorry that you have not passed the June exams. As a result we very much regret that you will not be able to enter the second year of the course. If you would like further information, please contact ...

It is still bad news but at least there is little more human spark in the second version!

Gender issues

What is the problem with this sentence?

> The student engineer needs to master calculus for his finals.

There are increasingly many female engineers. They will not be pleased if there is constant reference to the engineer as 'he'. In this case the best practice is to pluralize your main nouns; in that way you can then use 'they', which is non gender specific, for example

> Student engineers need to master calculus for their finals.

Paragraphs

A paragraph is a collection of sentences. In this collection the reader should be able to denote some linkage and some degree of relationship between them. The first sentence acts as a *topic sentence*; that is it introduces the topic or theme of the paragraph for the reader. It is a signpost. Busy readers in skimming through the text may simply read these topic sentences only and assume that they have gleaned the main theme of the paragraph. The topic sentence is quite clearly set out in this paragraph.

> Quality circles can be immensely useful in getting everyone involved in the organisation's drive for product improvement.

We are saying to our busy reader 'if you want further information about quality circles read on'. The important point is that as they read they can see the logical link between that topic sentence and the remainder of the paragraph. The advent of cut and paste has given us tremendous possibilities in being able to move sentences around from place to place. However we need to be careful that we don't break the linkage. Suppose after that topic sentence we pasted in this sentence about management.

> Quality circles can be immensely useful in getting everyone involved in the organisation's drive for product improvement. Management is often slow to realise just what effect a staff's lack of concern for quality can have on the product.

We present our reader with something of a puzzle. Why have we suddenly switched topic. Surely this new topic is rather different from that of the topic sentence. There appears to be no linkage phrase such as: *'This improvement is very much the concern of management; they are often slow'*. Readers to some extent predict what is coming next. If you use cut and paste a great deal and do not pay enough attention to the structure and linkage of the sentences then you will interfere with this prediction. This will have the effect of making your readers annoyed. They may stop reading or skim on to the next paragraph in the hope that it is easier to decode.

The author of this paragraph had decided to cut and paste extra material into it but he has been careful to secure the links.

> Quality circles can be immensely useful in getting everyone involved in the organisation's drive for product improvement. As far back as the 1940's, Edwards Deming, one of the pioneers of the quality movement, insisted that all workers should be involved from the start in the drive for total quality.

Notice how by using the phrase *'As far back as the 1940's'* the writer manages to link the topic sentence to the rest of the paragraph.

Inductive and deductive paragraph arrangements

You may have read some Sherlock Holmes stories. There the hero was always amazing his friend Dr Watson with brilliant feats of deduction.

> *'This man must have been a sailor, probably in the tropics, now owns a spaniel and lives near a water mill and plays the Welsh harp'.*

What Holmes was doing was making deductions from small but significant clues. A paragraph built round deductive structure follows the pattern: a thesis statement as topic sentence, for example

Total quality can never be achieved without sophisticated audit systems.

Then comes the 'proof', the reasoning that justifies that thesis.

Only through such auditing will all the many operations in the plant be tracked and their particular contribution to the product analysed. It is the auditing that can reveal deficiencies and short falls in quality. Nor can the job be done with any audit system; they have to be robust enough to detect quite small shifts in performance.

The inductive process is where the reasoning comes first and then it leads to the proof.

Quality is a difficult business; there are so many diverse and separate operations going on in any plant at any one time that it very difficult to keep track of them. Furthermore, when a break-down in quality occurs it is often equally difficult to spot exactly what has been responsible for it; there have been too many separate strands intertwined to enable a clear diagnosis to be carried out. So it is that sophisticated audit systems have to be built into the very foundations of the production process.

This kind of paragraph arrangement allows the writer to clinch the argument at the end after a series of proofs.

Editing your writing
When you have written your paragraphs and before you proof-read them for accuracy think about editing. This is a process whereby you tighten the writing, you try to eliminate unnecessary words and phrases. Remember, conciseness is a virtue.

Activity

Spend a few minutes editing this text. Compare your results with ours on the next page.

This survey aims to investigate the apparent very real decline in the use of sports facilities amongst undergraduate students on campus. Our investigation showed that many undergraduates felt that the sports facilities had become too expensive and therefore fewer had used them. We found that the discount system had not proved as popular as had been expected by the authorities. The report therefore recommends that better publicity for the sports facilities be adopted and that the forthcoming price rises are postponed until next year. (85 words)

Edited version

> This survey investigates the apparent decline in the use of sports facilities amongst undergraduates on campus. Many feel that these facilities have become too expensive, therefore fewer use them. The discount system has not proved as popular as had been expected. This report recommends that better publicity for the sports facilities be adopted and forthcoming price rises are postponed until next year. (62 words)

Comment

A reduction from 85 to 62 words.
A change from the past tense to the present for greater immediacy.

Using short forms: abbreviations, contractions and acronyms

Definitions

In engineering you will be using a number of short forms. Let us define the differences. An *abbreviation* is a short form, e.g. stands for 'for example' and i.e. stands for 'that is'. Oct. is an abbreviation and therefore should have a full stop. A *contraction* is a word which has been squashed such as Mr for Mister, Dr for Doctor. An *acronym* is a word composed of the initial letters of the name of something, e.g., NATO, AIDS.

Suggestions for use

- When you are in any doubt at all that your reader may not understand your use of a short form then do spell it out in your text.
- Always spell it out the first time you use the short form, e.g. the automatic gain control (agc) is provided in all sets
- Do provide a glossary.
  A list of all your short forms – so that your readers can have easy access to the forms you are using. Many glossaries can be found at the end of documents but you might like to consider that if you were the reader you might like to have such a list provided at the front to let you know what was coming up!
- Be consistent in the use of your short forms.
  We saw on page 162 that in specification writing we should be consistent with our forms; i.e. for hard disk not HD on one page and Hd Dk on the other; this applies to all our written work as engineers, consistency is crucial.

- Don't use one short form immediately after another. e.g. 'These computers are standard with the RAF; USAF forces however ...'
- Avoid redundancies with short forms, e.g. *dc (notice not CAPS) not dc current.*
- Avoid using full stops inside or directly after the short form except when you end a sentence.
- More, less
  < less than, ≮ not less than.
  > more than, ≯ not more than.

Standards

ISO = International Standards Organization has three parts to it.
BS = British Standards equivalents
ISO 9001/BS 5750 Part 1 – Most comprehensive, this would cover all research and development contracts.
ISO 9002/BS 5750 Part 2 – Most common in process industries.
ISO 9003/BS 5750 Part 3 – Least comprehensive. Used where product can be completely verified at the end of the process.

Writing numbers and symbols

You will be using numbers a great deal in your work.

Exercise

See how many of these you can identify. Answers below.

Units

metre	kelvin	kilogram	ampere	second
radian	volt	newton	hertz	joule
watt	ohm	pascal	farad	coulomb
litre	hectare	kilo		

Multiples of units

| kilo | mega | giga |

| Lower limit | Upper limit |

Answers

These are the standard SI units and their standard abbreviations.

Units

metre m	kelvin K	kilogram kg	ampere A	second s
radian rad	volt V	newton N	hertz Hz	joule J
watt W	ohm Ω	pascal Pa	farad F	coulomb C
litre l	hectare ha	kilo k		

Multiples of units

kilo k	mega M	giga G

Lower limit LL   Upper limit UL

Understanding and using the Greek alphabet

Many symbols used in engineering are Greek letters. It is important that you gain increasing acquaintance with these. They are used internationally. Figure 21.1 shows them as a full set: lower-case, capitals and as words. Greek letters are also used to represent quantities, see Figure 21.2.

Greek alphabet

α	A	alpha	ν	N	nu
β	B	beta	ξ	Ξ	xi
γ	Γ	gamma	o	O	omicron
δ	Δ	delta	π	Π	pi
ε	E	epsilon	ρ	P	rho
ζ	Z	zeta	σ	Σ	sigma
η	H	eta	τ	T	tau
θ	Θ	theta	υ	Y	upsilon
ι	I	iota	φ	Φ	phi
κ	K	kappa	χ	X	chi
λ	Λ	lambda	ψ	Ψ	psi
μ	M	mu	ω	Ω	omega

Figure 21.1

Greek letters are used to represent electric and magnetic quantities

ψ	–	Electric flux	–	Coulomb
Φ	–	Magnetic flux	–	Weber
ρ	–	Resistivity	–	Ohm metre
μ	–	Permeability	–	Henry per metre
λ	–	Wavelength	–	metre

Figure 21.2

Example of using the Greek alphabet

Standard form of equation of motion in a control system

$$\frac{d^2\theta_o}{dt^2} + 2\zeta\omega_n \frac{d^2\theta_o}{dt} + \omega_n^2\theta_o = \omega_n^2\theta_i$$

Figure 21.3

Writing equations

Some equations will be written using Greek letters. Figure 21.3 is an example.

Try always to write your equations on separate lines. Aim to number each equation in brackets on the right-hand side of your page and refer to them by that number. Make sure that your reader knows what letters, symbols, etc. you are using, for example:

When beam is loaded so that it bends only in plane of applied movement, stress distribution and curvature of beam are related by:

$$\frac{M}{I} = \frac{f}{y} = \frac{E}{R} \tag{1}$$

where M is the bending movement
I is the moment of inertia
E is the modulus of elasticity
R is the radius of curvature
f is the bending stress at distance y

Also to show that curvature of beam I/R can be given by

$$\frac{I}{R} = \frac{M}{EI} \tag{2}$$

The language of examinations

To some students the language used by examiners is every bit as strange as that of the Greek alphabet! Engineers both as students and in practice do not write many examinations and therefore we haven't devoted a separate section on this aspect in this book. However, if you do find yourself sitting an exam then do consider very "Caerphilly" what the examiners are trying to get at.

Here is glossary of terms which we hope you will find useful:

Explain: This is the most straightforward question. You need to demonstrate your understanding in a clearly structured account. Unless informed otherwise you can assume that you are writing to a competent engineer who will be familiar with the technical, mathematical languages you need,

Explain how boundary value problems can be solved by using appropriate Green's function.

Discuss: You must present to your reader an analysis – as thorough as you can – of the question. You must try and examine as many sides of the argument as possible. Very often you will be presented with a quotation:

Engineers increasingly should increasingly be trained away from the academic environment and in a practical way through placement with real engineers doing real engineering. Discuss.

You will get very little credit from the examiners if you simply take one side of this argument, i.e. that universities are doing a great job and engineering companies could not possibly take over this role. You will need to demonstrate an awareness of many of the criticisms that academic training through the BEng does not prepare engineers for the real world. You should mention recent reforms undertaken by universities via student placements, projects, etc. to ensure than degree courses do involve students in practical and 'real life' engineering.

Compare: Here you will need to present the similarities and differences as between the features mentioned in the question, e.g.:

Compare the quality control systems as adopted by leading US manufacturers such as Boeing with those used in the Japanese motor industry.

Very often you are asked to **compare and contrast.** In this case you would need to ensure that you brought out those features of the US and Japanese systems which are similar and those which are different. It is always essential to provide examples; vague general statements are seldom given much credit by examiners. You should also try and provide examples from your own reading and experience and not just relay on those from handouts and notes supplied by the lecturer or the key textbook.

Critically examine: Here you must state the pros and cons of the issue raised. Your final decision must rest on evidence. You will need to state clearly the reasons why you accept or reject any argument, e.g.:

Critically examine the proposition that all engineering students should learn at least one internationally used language.

Evaluate: Here you will need to make an informed judgement as to the relative value of the feature(s) mentioned, e.g.:

Evaluate the success of attempts by the UK governments following the Rio Conference to limit damage to the ozone layer.

To win examiners' approval you will need to demonstrate that you have enough background knowledge and understanding of the key issues to make an informed judgement. This is more difficult to do than simply compare and contrast.

So read the examination question carefully. Pay particular attention to the actual invitation used. Good luck.

Further reading

N J Higham (1993) *Handbook of Writing for the Mathematical Sciences.* SIAM (Philadelphia).
K Judd (1995) *Copyediting: A Practical Guide.* Robert Hale.

Index